SIN AND SELF-CONSCIOUSNESS IN THE THOUGHT OF FRIEDRICH SCHLEIERMACHER

SIN AND SELF-CONSCIOUSNESS

IN THE THOUGHT

OF FRIEDRICH SCHLEIERMACHER

NABPR Dissertation Series, Number 11

By
Robert Lee Vance

Published for
The National Association of Baptist Professors of Religion
by
The Edwin Mellen Press
Lewiston/Queenstown/Lampeteer

BX
4827
.S3
V36
1994

Library of Congress Cataloging-in-Publication Data

Vance, Robert Lee.
　　Sin and self-consciousness in the thought of Friedrich Schleiermacher / by Robert Lee Vance.
　　　　p.　　cm.
　　Includes bibliographical references.
　　ISBN 0-7734-2862-3
　　1. Schleiermacher, Friedrich, 1768-1834.　2. Sin.　3. Self-consciousness.　I. Title.
BX4827.S3V36　1995
233--dc20　　　　　　　　　　　　　　　　　　　　　　　　　94-40517
　　　　　　　　　　　　　　　　　　　　　　　　　　　　　　CIP

A CIP catalog record for this book is available from the British Library.

National Association of Baptist Professors of Religion
　　Senior Editor: Rollin S. Armour, Sr., Mercer University
Journal
　　Perspectives in religious Studies
　　　　Editor:　　R. Alan Culpepper, Baylor University
Series
　　Monograph Series
　　　　Editor:　　Edgar V. McKnight, Furman University
　　Dissertation Series
　　　　Editor:　　James Wm. McClendon, Jr., Fuller Theological Seminary
　　Bibliographic Series
　　　　Editor:　　David M. Scholer, North Park Theological Seminary

Copyright © 1994 The Edwin Mellen Press
All rights reserved. For information contact

The Edwin Mellen Press　　　　　　　　　　The Edwin Mellen Press
　　　Box 450　　　　　　　　　　　　　　　　　　　Box 67
　Lewiston, New York　　　　　　　　　　　Queenston, Ontario
　　USA 14092-0450　　　　　　　　　　　　CANADA L0S 1L0
　　　　　　　　　　The Edwin Mellen Press, Ltd.
　　　　　　　　　　Lampeter, Dyfed, Wales
　　　　　　　　　UNITED KINGDOM SA48 7DY

Printed in the United States of America

TABLE OF CONTENTS

Chapter 1: THE DOCTRINE OF SIN AND THE DOCTRINE OF PIETY . 1

Chapter 2: THE IMPLICIT STRUCTURAL ELEMENTS OF IMMEDIATE
SELF-CONSCIOUSNESS 17
- Introduction 17
  - Philosophical and Theological Perspectives on Immediate Self-Consciousness 17
  - The Ontological Status of Immediate Self-Consciousness 26
- World-Consciousness 34
  - The Strength of Influence by the World-Consciousness 34
  - World-Consciousness as Receptive and Active in its Knowing and Being towards the World 36
  - Reciprocity between Self and World in the Sensible Self-Consciousness 37
  - Sensible Self-Consciousness as the Realm of Antithesis between Self and Another 39
  - The Contrast between World-Consciousness and God-Consciousness 40
  - The Manifold Relativity of World-Consciousness 42
  - The Actual Precedence of World-Consciousness 45
  - The Predominance of World-Consciousness as Leading to Sin 48
- God-Consciousness 50

- God-Consciousness as a Structural Component in the Ontology of Existence 50
- The Qualitative Difference of God-Consciousness from World-Consciousness in Reference to Source 53
- God-Consciousness as Maintaining Self and World as Totally Different from God 55
- The God-Consciousness as Able to Comprehend the World-Consciousness 58
- The Philosophically Absolute Category of the "Transcendental Ground" 60
- The Absolute Qualitative Distinction between the Feeling-Self and the Transcendental One 62
- The Conjunction of God-Consciousness and World-Consciousness within the Actual Self-Consciousness as Not Implying an Identity of the Two Sources of Consciousness 67

Actual Self-Consciousness 70
- Introduction to Actual Self-Consciousness 70
- The Ontological Status of Actual Feeling 74
- Actual Existence as the Becoming of the Self's Reality 80
- Actuality as the Conjunctive Formalization of Potentials ... 84
- The Coeval, Coexistent Conjunction of the Two Potencies in Actuality 87
- The Actual Domination of Every Moment by One or the Other Potency 91
- The Dislocation of Actual Moments Leading to the Actuality of Sin 94

Chapter 3: THE STAGES OF DEVELOPMENT IN ACTUAL
          SELF-CONSCIOUSNESS 99
    Introduction 99
        States and Stages of the Actual Self-Consciousness 99
        The Processing of States into Stages of Actual
            Self-Consciousness 105
        The Antithesis of Pleasure and Pain in Every Moment
            of Actual Self-Consciousness 109
        The Antithesis of Sin and Grace in the Developing
            Stages of Actual Self-Consciousness 112
        The Factors of Determinism and Freedom in the Development
            of Actual Self-Consciousness 116
        Reflections on the Stages of Existence as Carried Out
            by Philosophy and Theology 123
    Original Co-Determination by World-Consciousness and
        God-Consciousness 125
        The Coexistence of the Potencies in a Primeval State 125
        The Tendency toward Domination by World-Consciousness
            as Original Sin 128
        The Tendency toward Domination by God-Consciousness
            as Original Perfection 132
        The Co-Equality of Original Sin and Original Perfection
            Becoming Actually Tilted Toward Sin 138
    The Predominance of World-Consciousness as the Actual State
        of Sin 146
        The Reality of Sin as a State of Actual
            Self-Consciousness 146
        The Dominance of World-Consciousness as Actual Sin ... 149
        The Suppression of God-Consciousness in Sin as the
            Incipient Impartation of Grace 155

  The Predominance of God-Consciousness as the Actual State
   of Grace 167
    The Reality of Grace as a State of Actual Self-
     Consciousness 167
    The Reality of Grace as Communicated by the Redeemer . 173
    The Suppression of World-Consciousness in Grace as the
     Consciousness of Sin 177
    The Dominance of God-Consciousness in Grace as the
     Consciousness of Redemption 185

Chapter 4: CONCLUDING EVALUATION: THE PLACE OF THE
  DOCTRINE OF SIN IN SCHLEIERMACHER'S
  SYSTEM OF THOUGHT 191
  Introduction 191
  The Starting Point of Dialectical Understanding: Creation
   or Redemption 195
  Determinism and Freedom: How Schleiermacher's System
   Logically Entails Sin 200
  Feeling as Freedom: Its Conceptual Adequacy in a
   Deterministic System 204
  The Perfect Determination of Actual Self-Consciousness
   in Christ 209

SELECTED BIBLIOGRAPHY 215

NABPR DISSERTATION SERIES 221

CHAPTER 1

THE DOCTRINE OF SIN AND THE DOCTRINE OF PIETY

Contemporary theological discussions often find a convenient point of historicalreference in the thought of Friedrich Schleiermacher, basically because in his oft-acknowledged role as "father of modern theology" he is seen as having introduced the peculiarly modern understanding of the paradox of transcendentally-perfect creator God and existentially-sinful creature humanity. In quite substantive ways, moreover, most modern theologians acknowledge debts to Schleiermacher, and feel it both necessary and appropriate to compare their ideas, whether *pro* or *con*, with those of their forbear. The pivotal issue in Schleiermacher's system, and because of him, in much of modern theology, is usually seen to be the relation of God's being to humanity's being—with the ontological issue bearing intrinsically upon the epistemological issue, of how the divine reality may be known within the terms of human consciousness.

The very assertion that the divine being may be encountered somehow within the confines of the human being seems to lead, however, to the allowance that the divine may be not just contained, but also counteracted, by the human consciousness, in a seemingly inevitable outcome of sin. For most interpreters of Schleiermacher, therefore, it is the basic context of consciousness that poses a question of the essential seriousness of the doctrines of both God and sin. It is seldom as apparent, however, that an examination of the entire problematic of human consciousness may reveal a sense of mutually-implicative seriousness in the two doctrines, and that a serious understanding of sin at that basic level may redound conversely to a better understanding of God.

The reason that sin presents itself so eminently as a critical point in deciphering Schleiermacher's conceptual system is that it functions for him as a properly equivocal term, with usages both in a philosophical sense and in a theological sense. In his religio-philosophical analysis of the structure of human consciousness, sin designates a completely enveloping state of worldliness in the actual self-consciousness, the true dimensions of which are only obliquely apparent to the confused reflections of the sinful self. The actual state of "sin," therefore, is able to have only a veiled awareness of its further implicit reference to the subsequent state of "piety," in which sin will be seen only as a presupposed opposition to the dominance of God-consciousness. This derivative meaning of sin, in the state of pious consciousness, is expressed in the transmuted terminology of the theological perspective as the sin that is redeemed-by-grace, and experienced then only as a "consciousness-of-sin," as an indirect retrospection on a preliminary but now ineffectual state of being. It is nonetheless clear that for Schleiermacher, the originative factual identity of the actual state of "sin" *per se* is always the same, whether it is being described intrinsically and directly by philosophy, or extrinsically and retrospectively by theology.

The aims and approaches of philosophy and theology can thus be shown for Schleiermacher to be parallel, even if distinct, for each is a theoretical analysis of similar empirical data of basic human experience. The difference lies in the end of the spectrum of experience upon which each focuses its description of the life process: philosophy begins at the foundational, originative end to describe the generally structural conditions of human existence, and theology begins at the culminative end of the spectrum to describe the final, integrative state into which existence may be transformed. The reason that "sin" is a more multivocal and suggestive term for Schleiermacher's entire system of thought than is "piety," lies in the fact that piety, or the actually dominant consciousness of God, is only realized as the final possible stage of human existence, while sin is endemically realized even from the beginning stages, and provides the necessary backdrop for the actual accession of God-consciousness in the culminative stage of redemption. Sin is seen as mankind's original self-actualizing state of world-orientation, as a self-derived exercise intrinsically open to our general philosophical reflection.

Piety, on the other hand, is the phenomenon that simply occurs within mankind as the given reassertion of divine presence previously obscured, and is thereby understood by humans only to the limited degree of our capacity to accept it and to orient ourselves to it. In the philosophical analysis of the phenomenon of sin, sin is identified as that state of consciousness that universally obtains to prevent the multifarious feelings of worldly existence from attaining the ultimate and unified meaning that only piety reveals. From a theological analysis, sin must then be seen as having been but a stage of attentuated realization of God's presence to human existence, and must be recognized by faith as but an implicit precursor of the now theologically central experience of dominant God-consciousness.

The methodological question that has thus presented itself more to his critics than it did to Schleiermacher has been whether sin is essentially an ethical term of philosophical concern, or a religious term of theological concern. Schleiermacher's implicit answer to the question indeed reveals how and why sin is such an instructively equivocal term for him: in the overall scope of his thought, Schleiermacher indicates that there is no substantive difference between the concerns of philosophical ethics and of theological piety. The basic realities of human existence are for both the common matters of concern, but they differ in their forms of approach to these matters. All phenomena in the whole range of human life may be taken for analysis by either discipline, but each is more focused upon a particular stage of life—either before or after the dominance of God-consciousness—so that it considers the other stage mainly by implication and reflection.

The stage of sin is seen by Schleiermacher as the original and utterly universal condition of mankind, and as best focused upon by philosophy's generalizing approach to the immanentally-known structure of human nature. Even though philosophy does indeed become attentive to religion whenever that transcendental-ly-originated state of self-consciousness becomes actualized, it nevertheless engages in the philosophy of religion only as an extension of its general interest in the primal actualization of the structures of consciousness. Because sin is acknowledged by all humans either implicitly or explicitly as their original self-actualization, it becomes the focus of philosophy's examination of humanity. Philosophy in its openness to the truth of life must therefore point to sin, or to some confused sense of it, as a continuous factor in life, whether as the outright actualization of the original stage, or as the presupposed basis for the subsequent stage of piety.

The stage of piety, of existence focused on God rather than on the world, is a more singular state simply because only some people become thus transformed by the ingression of divine power. Theology is concerned to examine and to describe only this specifically culminating stage of life under the true aegis and power of God-consciousness. Theology is therefore able to look at the previous stage of dominant world-consciousness, or sin, *only* at a remove, that is, through the eyes of the redeemed self-consciousness. Within the terminology of pious theology, therefore, "sin" has a definite but oblique connotation: piety does have a "consciousness *of* sin" as its presuppositional and actual antecedent, but it can no longer comprehend "sin" *per se* as an entire state of the consciously existing self.

Because of the fact that God-consciousness must become dominant before one can see the actual limitations to which dominant world-consciousness has subjected the self, the originally non-pious, worldly self cannot explicitly realize *in situ*, or acknowledge in its ethical-philosophical reflections, that it is religiously in a state of sin. Only the subsequently pious self will be able to broaden the horizons of philosophical reflection to pursue a philosophy of religion, and thereby be able to point out precisely how and why the self's former sinful interests were limited to the worldly parameters of consciousness, in exclusion of the God-consciousness. A connotational examination of the meaning of sin in each may be for Schleiermacher the basis for indicating a typology of the two stages of life, as they are at once distinguished and linked as successive operations of the fundamental self-consciousness. This interplay and mutual suggestiveness of the two dominant stages of human life may in turn indicate for Schleiermacher a model of how philosophy and theology operate theoretically both as related and as distinct.

Schleiermacher's designation of sin as the endemic characteristic state of humanity in our primal stage of conscious life, and of piety as the characteristic state of the gracefully effected subsequent stage of life, indicates the underlying connectedness of the two, as contrasting but reciprocal modes of our basal existence in self-conscious feeling. This connection indicates that for Schleiermacher sin and piety are opposing but mutually-presupposing potential states of the same actually conscious self. The two are understood as connected in such concretely reciprocal fashion that they may be analyzed conceptually to reflect a similarly reciprocal understanding of the connectedness of philosophy and theology.

Conceptual analysis must work in *philosophy* to define sin as that incomplete state of life that strives to project for itself a worldly unity and focus within actual consciousness. But with a sense of reciprocal relatedness, as well as distinction, conceptual analysis must work in *theology* to describe piety as that integrated state in which the misaligned intentions of sin are overcome and redirected by divine transformation. In the overall proceedings of his systematic thought, Schleiermacher therefore implicitly suggests the mutual interconnectedness of sin and piety by pointing up the mutual suggestiveness of all philosophical and theological reflection upon them. But in light of the fact that sin is the earlier and more continuous of the two states of life, it may be taken as having more quantitative ramification in conceptualizing human development, and thus as having a terminological ubiquity and equivocity that piety does not exemplify.

The way in which sin functions as a term of similar but equivocal reference through both actual stages of life generates insight additionally into the way in which Schleiermacher uses his most fundamental category of consciousness, that of "feeling." Indeed, because "sin" *per se* indicates the earlier state of dominance by world-consciousness over God-consciousness in the actually self-conscious feeling, and because "consciousness *of* sin" indicates the subsequently pious state of their complete reversal in actual consciousness, the two usages of "sin" can suggest a general model of the underlying operation of actual consciousness, or feeling, as a whole. It is because of both the material and the formal ramifications that sin suggests in the overall pattern of Schleiermacher's thought, that this study will seek to discover through sin new insights into the meaning of its reciprocal state of piety, and a new sense of the seriousness with which Schleiermacher regarded both.

Sin will consequently be seen along with piety as an actual state of immediate self-consciousness, or feeling, and it will be in examining these two contrasting modes that we hope finally to come to an understanding of "feeling," as the most crucial and most difficult of all Schleiermacher's terms. Because feeling is usually regarded as being such a problematic concept, it will be hoped that in gaining an understanding of the particular meaning and reality of both sin and piety, that a new sense of the full dimensionality of feeling will also be gained. Friend and foe alike have recognized that feeling, as Schleiermacher's most critical term, raises fundamentally serious questions of epistemology, and ultimately also of ontology. Most of the attention, moreover, has been placed on piety in particular as the distinctive state of feeling, with the basic questions usually raised in terms of just what the particular pious feeling of absolute dependence can claim to know and claim to be. It will be the effort of this study, however, to examine the sinful state of feeling as the precursor of the pious, or graceful, state, and by demonstrating the material differences between the two, thereby to reveal their formal similarities as fully real and fully knowing states of actual self-consciousness, or feeling.

The elucidation of this formal similarity will then be seen as confirmation of Schleiermacher's basically inductive, or empirical, approach to the study of humanity's conscious existence. All reflection on the nature of consciousness begins with descriptions of specific, actual moments of conscious existence, but these will be found only as instances of one or another of the two general states of consciousness, that is, either of sin or of piety. From these specific moments, reflection can then proceed phenomenologically to a more general analysis of the two states of consciousness as modes of the underlying structure of actual existence, and from there to an ontological analysis of the place of human existence in the whole of being. But throughout the processes of reflection, whether from the view of philosophy or the view of theology, Schleiermacher maintains that the specific content of the actually conscious states must be defined as either sinful or graceful moments. The interplay of sin and grace in the continuing process of existence will be seen as the entire potential constitution of every human life, and thereby as the given empirical basis for any religio-philosophical construction of the terms of human ontology.

The main line of criticism advanced by Schleiermacher's detractors has undoubtedly been that which focuses on the questionability of feeling as an adequately substantive category of either epistemology or ontology. It will be our effort to elucidate and finally to deflect much of that criticism, by demonstrating that both specific types of feeling—sinful feeling and pious feeling—exemplify for Schleiermacher the full reality and cognizance that can be entailed in a fundamental state of actual feeling. Critiques of Schleiermacher's view of sin-feeling have usually gone hand in hand with critiques of his view of pious-feeling, and it seems now a pertinent means for re-evaluating his view of piety to review its formal and material categorial links to sin.

The most trenchant of Schleiermacher's critics, in the neo-orthodox school of the second quarter of the twentieth century, have indeed seen the appropriateness of such a connection, for in perceiving Schleiermacher through the nineteenth-century's attenuated version of him, they have reacted against what they saw as his subjectivization of religion and his consequent trivialization of sin. In reversing this analytical sequence, we may now hope in first demonstrating the strong seriousness of his view of sin, to allow that concept to redound to a more incisive understanding of religion itself.

Schleiermacher's most eminent critic, Karl Barth, pointed out the connection between religion and sin in his critical estimate that for Schleiermacher religion was an anthropomorphic reflexiveness, and sin a failure to project God in man's "teleological" effort to transcend that subjective reflection.[1] Barth believed that Schleiermacher postulated religion, or piety, more as a human faculty than as a divine impartation, and that sin was consequently the failure of man's best efforts to live up to his own ideal of himself. In so interpreting Schleiermacher's doctrine of human self-consciousness as idealistically reflexive, Barth effectively categorized Schleiermacher with a Fichtean-type of cognitive egocentrism. The underlying reason for Schleiermacher's "anthropocentric" approach to religion and to sin was what Barth considered to be his artificially enforced collapsing of theology into philosophy in the fundamentally self-conscious category of feeling. It will therefore be our effort here to reconsider sin and piety as the distinctively actualized states of feeling, in order that we may re-establish the seriousness with which Schleiermacher intended them to convey the actual involvement of human feeling with the realities of world and God lying beyond it.

Emil Brunner proposed a different line of criticism of Schleiermacher, but still grounded it in the basic neo-orthodox charge of Schleiermacher's subjectivization of religion. Brunner believed that Schleiermacher's definition of piety as the feeling of absolute dependence really indicates a mystical-pantheistic participation in the divine, and is so plainly passive that it can be reduced to an essentially

---

[1]Karl Barth, *Protestant Thought: From Rousseau to Ritschl* (New York: Simon and Schuster, 1959) 317.

subjective state of receptivity.[2] This emphasis on receptivity, according to Brunner, is really an extension of the Platonic tradition of ontologism, in which the self is seen as the finite representative of, or participant in, infinite spirit. The meaning of sin for Schleiermacher thereby is interpreted as the inability to tune out all active, or "teleological," intentions from the passive subject's immersion in its spiritual matrix. In this regard, Brunner would emphasize the kinship of Schleiermacher with his romantic rather that his idealist milieu, such as the type of "rational intuitionism" found in Jacobi's theory of immediate subjective knowledge of spiritual realities. Such a mystical blurring of self and God is Brunner's version of the subjectivization that he attributes to Schleiermacher, even though in a rather different vein than Barth.

The common burden that Barth and Brunner bear against Schleiermacher is quite evidently what they perceive as his subjectivization of faith, or in terms of theological positioning, his immanentizing of God. The very fact, however, that these two critics see different tendencies of Schleiermacher as evidence of what both would call a subjectivistic immanentism, seems to indicate that there is in Schleiermacher more dynamic, and perhaps also more implicit substance, than their respectively single-minded critiques would allow. The active sort of Fichtean self-projection perceived by Barth is quite different from the passive sort of Jacobian receptivity seen by Brunner, and a further examination of Schleiermacher's theory of the religious self might indicate that the subject is able to exercise both postures of existence only because of its relationships to objective axes of being.

Indeed, a historical analysis of Schleiermacher's intellectual milieu would reveal that he deliberately sought to position himself beyond many of the accepted theories of both the idealist and the romanticist sort. Although he may have absorbed more of the subjectivism of Fichte than he realized, he clearly defined

---

[2]Emil Brunner, *Die Mystik und das Wort* (Tübingen: J.C.B. Mohr, 1924) 35-77. Also, by the same author, *Revelation and Reason*, trans. Olive Wyon (Philadelphia: Westminster Press, 1946) 350-52, 398.

it in other than idealist or cognitivist categories. And while he did feel a genuine personal sympathy with Jacobi's struggle to maintain the prerogatives of immediate intuition, he did not allow it to devolve into mysticism or immanentism.

Schleiermacher's view of immediate self-consciousness sought to define consciousness more in ontological-existential terms than in epistemological terms as a means of affirming the transcendental self, not as a preclusive integer, but as a distinct adjunct of the further transcendental realities of God and world. Self-consciousness for Schleiermacher was the self's way of re-having itself, of affirming its transcendental determinations by together knowing and being the self-as-determined. Self-consciousness is thus taken out of the introspective tradition in which most idealism and romanticism had located it, for they make the self reflect upon itself in some sort of mentalistic self-determination. Self-consciousness is for Schleiermacher not an introspective knowledge of one's own mental states, but is rather the being-knowing affirmation of the whole self in its transcendental givenness. For Schleiermacher, the self simply finds itself as "given" by its metaphysical determinations, not as "thinking" or "feeling" them into being out of it own prerogatives.

Indeed, the feeling self is seen by Schleiermacher as existing precisely between the external poles of God and world, and it is only by affirming its absolute determination that the self can properly comprehend its relative feelings of determination by the world. Absoluteness is thus reflected in the religious self quite as much as is relativity, and sin is reckoned by Schleiermacher as the gauge that shows just how serious can be the actual self-assertive revolt by the finite world-consciousness against the reciprocal consciousness of the infinite determination of the whole of being.

The explanation of Schleiermacher's view of the seriousness of sin as more than an internal confusion of subjective consciousness will thereby aid in a further demonstration of the external origin of the element that he finds as determinative of the state of religious consciousness. The actual state of sin, as the self's immanental immersion in worldly feelings to the exclusion of the transcendentally derived feelings of absolute dependence, serves as the obverse demonstration of what the reverse state of grace will reveal as the reality of absolute determination having awaited its actualization within human consciousness. Going through the horns of Schleiermacher's supposed transcendental-immanental dilemma, we may propose that a transcendental analysis of the immanental state of sin can serve as an instructive entree into a re-evaluation of Schleiermacher's mature definition of the state of religion, as the divine action of grace imparting itself to the sinful human consciousness.

In accordance with Schleiermacher's position, we would need follow neither the transcendentalistic neo-conservatives—such as Barth and Brunner—nor the immanentalistic neo-culturalists—such as the existentialists who claim God is man, the natural theologians who claim God is the world, or the hermeneutical-phenomenologists who proclaim God in the social matrix of consciousness. We know God, says Schleiermacher, because the conquest of sin in our experience of divine grace reveals God as absolutely determinative of humanity: both of its essential selfhood and of its existing-feeling, conscious self. We must therefore understand God neither as completely transcendent, as in the neo-orthodox tendency for dualism, nor as completely immanent, as in the neo-cultural tendency for monism. The self-destructive status of sin within human consciousness is reckoned as drastically real because of the contrasting status of transforming grace that reveals existentially to each human the continuing determination of the God who has in reality upheld the *essential* life of the person throughout both the sinful and graceful states of *existence*.

If Schleiermacher's doctrine of sin demonstrates that the alien state of consciousness is indeed substantively "other" than the ideal, by the same token, the doctrine of piety shows that the graceful state of consciousness reveals the definitive activity of the absolutely "other" God. Schleiermacher may thus be seen as steering a middle course between the monistic immanentism often attributed to him and the transcendental dualism that Barth and the dialectical school thought so far beyond him. That Schleiermacher was conscious of the possibility of his thought being interpreted as immanental or pantheistic was shown in his studious but unrelenting denials of the charges of "Spinozism" levelled at him, especially in the early part of his career. Such interpretations should have been laid to rest by Schleiermacher's progressively more definitive explications of self-consciousness as transcendentally oriented toward sources beyond itself, but his critics and finally many of his followers chose to interpret him through the mystical-romantic and idealist views that were coming into favor around Schleiermacher.

Much of nineteenth-century theology, indeed, was to follow this subjectivist-immanentist view of Schleiermacher, so that by the end of that era the prevailing presentations of Schleiermacher made him seem the father of every sort of immanentism, whether liberalism, existentialism, or historicist phenomenology. It was through the eyes of Schleiermacher's putative followers, therefore, that the neo-conservative movement came to see him, and it was against this undoubtedly immanental version of his teachings that they came to reassert the transcendental objectivism of their dialectical theology. These neo-conservative thinkers and their present-day followers—who now view Schleiermacher through the eyes of Bultmann, Tillich, and Braun, rather than through Ritschl, Dilthey, and Otto—might best be able to re-evaluate Schleiermacher's emphasis on the transcendental source of religion if they could first re-evaluate his view of sin as man's immanental, but actually fateful, disruption of the transcendental providence.

In terms of traditional considerations of the concept of human evil, Schleiermacher will be seen to define sin as more substantive than a mere privation of good, as in immanental monism, but as less radical than the dichotomous fall of transcendental dualism. Although Schleiermacher did have affinities with the neo-Platonic tradition of monism, he was concerned on many occasions to affirm that the creation of humanity's finite being was not the origin of evil, in any sort of existential attenuation of emanating being. In this regard, he was especially anxious to disavow the Spinozistic view of evil as a mere illusion, or mental entity, within the comprehensive monism, for this would have placed humankind ontologistically within the same immanent sphere as God. On the other hand, he did not wish to extrapolate from human sin such a metaphysically radical view of evil that a dualistically subsisting counterforce to God would be adduced.

After examining and reworking the various antecedent views of evil, Schleiermacher finally came to the view that evil is a human reality, in the ontologically-existentially relative sphere of self-consciousness, and that it may consequently be deemed as a metaphysical nothing (*Nichts*) only in a transcendental comparison with the absolute metaphysical priority of divine determination. Humanity's sin is thus the situation of his knowing-being self so existing that his world-consciousness is actualized in dominance over his God-consciousness, and piety is the reversal of this state within existence by God's graceful empowering of humanity's God-consciousness into dominant actualization instead. The intricate presuppositions and ramifications of this view for the formulas of traditional theology were profound, but nowhere more so than in their implications for the concepts of God's grace and human redemption.

The state of sin can now be seen as both the logically necessary and the ontologically actual antecedent of the state of piety, because for Schleiermacher sin must be resolved only in piety. Piety is seen, therefore, not as a "natural tendency," as Bultmann was to say, pre-understood innately by humans, but as the state of actualized consciousness as redeemed from sin by God's grace. The most continuing and relentless of all criticisms of Schleiermacher's thought has been that for him piety was a general faculty of the natural self-consciousness, and not a definite state of involvement with transcendent reality. Consequently, it is only by understanding it as a singularly actualized state of transformation from sin that piety can properly be seen as the divinely-imparted state of redemption, or grace. Just as sin is seen to have been the stage of dominant self-actualizing of the potential world-consciousness over the potential God-consciousness, redemption is seen as God's determinative empowering of that God-consciousness into actual domination instead. Our disruptive instantiation of sin as our actual mode of self-conscious life is resolved by God's responding instantiation of grace through the uniquely universal event of Christ, to empower our God-consciousness into full reality in the life of self-consciousness. Redemption could never be seen as a "growing perfection" of an innately powerful God-consciousness, or else there would be no explanation for God's revelation in Christ, as the specific means of transforming our self-consciousness from world-orientation to God-orientation.

As Schleiermacher developed the full implications of his theological system, he also made further philosophical efforts to point up the particularity of sin and piety as distinct and successive states of the actual self-consciousness, in contrast to the sort of generalized and immanentized states that many critics had discerned in his earlier philosophical writings. Piety, or religion, is therefore understood neither as an immanent capacity for self-developing perfection nor as a transcendentally implanted *Anknüpfungspunkt* of immediate participation with God. Rather, it is the divinely willed and imparted state of existentially actualizing our knowledge and love of God in response to the original absolute determination. The concept of piety thus indicates a state of existence somehow between purely subjective religion and a purely objective revelation. Correspondingly, the concept of sin, as piety's contrary antecedent, helps by material contrast to indicate structurally the sort of reality that piety exemplifies.

The only extended study of Schleiermacher's doctrine of sin in English, a dissertation by George N. Boyd entitled "The Doctrine of Original Sin and the Fall in the Theology of Friedrich Schleiermacher,"[3] seems too anxious to reinterpret Schleiermacher to satisfy the demands of neo-conservative thinkers on their own objectivistic terms. Boyd tries to point up the seriousness of sin for Schleiermacher by placing it intrinsically within the domain of *pious* consciousness, and then by assigning objective reference to both sin and piety as cognitively comprehensive of transcendent being. Boyd assumes that for Schleiermacher sin

---

[3]George N. Boyd, "The Doctrine of Original Sin and the Fall in the Theology of Friedrich Schleiermacher" (Th.D. dissertation, Union Theological Seminary, New York, 1970).

is a species of the generic feeling of God, rather than being the separate and opposite generic feeling of the world, with both being distinct, but alternately dominant, states of the feeling-self. Such a view as Boyd's compromises the real, though non-cognitive, objective reference that Schleiermacher saw as embodied in the respective states of sin and piety, and it must therefore be in first understanding the distinct locus and dynamic of each state that we come to understand their mutually implicative reality.

It is in light of Schleiermacher's continuous use of postulated definitions of the structural components and processing states of immediate self-consciousness, or feeling, that one must understand his ontological (or philosophical) explication of the place and function of sin and piety in consciousness. Because Boyd fails to place sin and religion in the correct framework of Schleiermacher's philosophy of existence, his entire study is confused by the assumption that sin is a specific type of instance within the general state of piety, and that only Schleiermacher's retrospectively pious theological explication of original sin is necessary for understanding their entire complex and equivocal relationship. A broader study of Schleiermacher's whole system of thought, therefore, will reveal substantially different conclusions about his understanding of the locus and dynamic of sin as humanity's world-oriented pre-emption of consciousness, and of the countervalent nature of piety as God's redemptive self-presentation.

A needed correction of the neo-orthodox interpretation of Schleiermacher as radically subjectivistic thus need not swing to such an interpretation as Boyd's, which holds Schleiermacher as objectivistic in the same cognitive-conceptual way by which neo-orthodoxy defines truth. A balanced interpretation of Schleiermacher should rather show him to have seen truth as objectively and subjectively composite in the uniquely human reality of feeling, with self-conscious feeling being both subjectively aware and objectively referential. The kind of objectivizing by which reference is made is not that of conceptual cognition, but is rather the more holistic personal comprehension of the being-knowing nexus in feeling. In order to be regarded as both ontologically real and epistemologically valid, feeling in Schleiermacher should not be seen with Barth as a romantically ephemeral emotionality chasing its own tail, but neither must it be seen with Boyd as a cognitively definite apprehension of trans-subjective being. The sense of reality and veracity contained in human feeling as indicated by Schleiermacher is instead comprehensive and expressive at the same time of both being and knowing.

Both piety and sin must therefore be seen as exemplifying the ontological comprehensiveness of an actual state of feeling. Sin-feeling must be regarded as a fully actual mode of the feeling-self, and to be as real in its opposition to the feeling of God as piety is real in its acceptance. Sin is as distinctly real a state of feeling as is its dialectical opposite of piety, and it cannot for Schleiermacher be subsumed as an attenuated sub-type of piety. Consequently, because sin is not located under piety, it cannot for Schleiermacher be considered as a proper subject of theological reflection, but must be considered in a hybrid framework of philosophy of religion that ties together theological phenomenology with philosophical ontology. Sin *per se* is explicated only by the humanistic ontology that focuses on the world-dominant state of feeling-self, whereas piety is viewed as the distinctly God-oriented state of feeling, uniquely described and delineated in theology. To attempt to view sin as an aspect of the pious state of dominant God-consciousness would therefore be to implicate sin as related more to God than to mankind. The confining of the full consideration of sin to a philosophy of mankind's entire religious existence is the way in which Schleiermacher emphasizes that sin is the necessarily general presupposition of the specifically determined state of piety. But it is only by considering their reciprocal status and functioning within the whole process of life-feeling that philosophy of religion can indicate how for Schleiermacher sin and piety are separate but mutually implicative stages along life's way.

CHAPTER 2

THE IMPLICIT STRUCTURAL ELEMENTS OF IMMEDIATE SELF-CONSCIOUSNESS

INTRODUCTION

Philosophical and Theological Perspectives on Immediate Self-Consciousness

In surveying Schleiermacher's overall system of thought, it can be seen that he thinks and expresses himself at certain times as a philosopher and at certain times as a theologian. Yet it also becomes apparent that he holds the two roles, or outlooks, only in relative distinction, and recognizes that with their differences they also bear real similarities. The most important similarity, certainly, would be that of subject matter, for Schleiermacher seems to realize that for all their hermeneutical and stylistic differences, the two disciplines both aim centrally to deal with the matters of human self-consciousness. In drawing the distinctions between them, therefore, Schleiermacher adduces basically methodological differences for delineation, while acknowledging the "immediate self-consciousness," or "feeling," as a common substantive ground of reality and knowledge. The differences of style and starting point may be suggested by the philosophical bent for general, substantive, ontological terminology, in contrast to the theological bent for concrete, experiential, functional terminology. These methodological approaches to the two disciplines by Schleiermacher may indeed betray a kind of hermeneutic underlying his entire thought, but only by entering into that complex of thought will we be able to determine his justification in establishing such a program.

We will undertake an examination of the concept of sin in regard to both its philosophical and its theological senses, realizing that as a definite phenomenon of the immediate self-consciousness, Schleiermacher's view of sin has material significance for both conceptual approaches to human life. Because sin is seen by Schleiermacher as an actual state of self-consciousness, one must understand both its ontological locus in consciousness for philosophy, and its existential functioning in consciousness for theology. We must keep in mind, however, that each perspective is for Schleiermacher a type of reflection upon the same actual situation of self-consciousness. This distinction between the two perspectival treatments of sin-in-consciousness will allow us, first, in this chapter, to examine the philosophical understanding of sin as a general human phenomenon, couched in the implicit ontological structure of immanently known self-consciousness. In the following chapter, we will then undertake a philosophy-of-religion treatment of the sin-in-consciousness, from the perspective of theologically specified piety, as it looks back philosophically on the state of sin as the blockage of the struggling God-consciousness.

Our order of consideration will therefore be, first, to sketch a structural (or *existenzial*, to use Heidegger's later term for the formal or ontological analysis of existence) model of the immediate self-consciousness, in order then to describe the structural elements concretely *in situ* of the actual (*existenziell, per* Heidegger) process of life in the human individual.[1] But for Schleiermacher there is a more

---

[1]The hermeneutical format in Schleiermacher's thinking may be seen as rather similar to that presented later by Heidegger, although Schleiermacher never actually adopts the terms "ontological" and "existential" for the two ends of the hermeneutical scale. His basic usage does, however, refer to the philosophical and the theological disciplines as being respectively general and specific in their treatments of human nature. In his *Brief Outline*, Schleiermacher thus speaks of the relatively theoretical approach of philosophy which must be dialectically informed by the relatively empirical approach of theology. In *The Christian Faith*, the generalized philosophical deductions about humanity are termed "presuppositional," which would seem basically comparable to Heidegger's term "onto-

intrinsic carryover from the one referential perspective to the other than there is for Heidegger: Heidegger concentrates so fully on the basic "ontology of *Dasein*" that he seldom portrays how actual moments of ambiguous existence contribute ontically to a better conceptualization of the elemental structure implicit in them. Schleiermacher, however, is constantly reassessing the ontological categories of conscious existence in light of the ever dynamic actualities of successive existential moments. As the interrelationships of the structural elements of existence manifest themselves in their cyclical flow of potentialities and actuality, Schleiermacher illustrates how their philosophically general schematization is validated only by their theologically specific exemplification in the actual moments of existence. Philosophy (or existential ontology) is thus seen as being no more primal nor definitive than is theology (as the phenomenology of pious moments), for both are seen as dealing with the same realities of conscious existence, if only from different starting points, and at different stages of insight into the context of human experience.

For Schleiermacher, therefore, the heuristic modelling of a structural ontology of existence is only a foundational starting point for a full phenomenology of existence, for the structure can truly be understood only in light of the ever developing interactions of its elements. From the theological perspective of reflection on pious moments of God-consciousness, the constitutive elements of an ontology of existence cannot be accurately ascertained and analyzed until after the graceful conclusion of the life's actual alternation between the elements of God-consciousness and world-consciousness. The qualitative difference between the two elemental *potentials* is never understood in

---

logical," or *existenzial*, in contrast to the specified phenomenology of existing moments to which both also refer.

Heidegger exemplifies in many ways the same interests and the same approaches as Schleiermacher, particularly in the focus on conscious existence as the primal ground of philosophy and of philosophy of religion. Heidegger's classic essay in combining philosophy and phenomenology is his *Sein und Zeit* (Halle: Max Niemeyer Verlag, 1927), and it is here by applying the generalizing modes of philosophy to the particular phenomena of human existence that he develops his seminal "ontology of *Dasein*."

philosophical terms, for only in the final stage of dominance by the God-consciousness does theology ascertain just what the *actual* self-consciousness has been mediating in the struggle between world-consciousness and God-consciousness.

Schleiermacher suggests that we come to a fully adequate philosophy of existence only *after* the empirical data of the life's existential development are recognized for what they are. (This develops in much the same way that Bultmann tries to maintain over against Heidegger that an ontology of existence is truncated or unfulfilled if it is not informed by actual experiences of existential significance.) Schleiermacher recognizes that a philosophy of existence can be fully accurate only if it comes also to include a philosophy of religious existence, and that this element of religious consciousness is presented *de facto* only in the culminative stage of life upon which theology must be focused. It must be said, therefore, that for Schleiermacher the ontology of general existence and the theology of pious existence are held as mutually informative, with both needing the insights and expressions of the other, but with neither assuming any final epistemological prerogative over the other.

When an ontology of existence is fully informed and conceived, it would purport for Schleiermacher to reflect the universally and originally given structure of every human self-consciousness, even though its elements and parameters are only grasped during the course of existential development. It is for this reason, apparently, that Schleiermacher himself is never interested in spelling out in one theoretical schema his entire ontology of existence. That he came to explicate one within his own mind, however, is quite apparent, for the elements of an implicit ontology are presented in various ways and in various locations in his writing, but usually as presuppositional formulae for certain theological reflections. It will be our task here to explicate more fully Schleiermacher's existential-ontological framework, but only by constantly referring it to, and adducing facts to illustrate it from particular instances of actual self-consciousness. "Actual self-consciousness," therefore, will serve as the conceptual linchpin between the two systematic frames of reference, for it will indicate both the *particular* momentary instantiations of immediate self-consciousness, or existence, and the ontological locus for such actual moments within the *universally* given structure of existence.

Especially in his systematic theological work, *The Christian Faith*, Schleiermacher develops his philosophy of consciousness as a hermeneutical basis for developing his theology of pious consciousness. It is the intermingling of the two sorts of terminology in that work—such as the originally philosophical concept of "immediate self-consciousness," and the originally theological concept of "sin"—which has led to so much confusion among both his friends and his critics. Yet it seems the inevitable outcome for a person who pursued dual roles as philosopher and as theologian, and who did indeed seek to point up their strong levels of correlative concern. In order, therefore, to understand exactly how and why Schleiermacher came in his *magnum opus* to presume such affinity and even cross-fertilization between the two disciplines, it would be necessary to trace the development of his philosophical-ontological treatments of the domain of human consciousness as they developed apace through the years of his growing theological development. It is not the purpose of this study to engage in such historical analysis, but it will be necessary for the more systematic purpose here to present at least examples and indications from his philosophical works of how he developed the implicit ontology of conscious existence which he sets out as preliminary to his final theological treatment. Some of these philosophical underpinnings have already been explored, as have some of their theological ramifications, but it will now be our task explicitly to outline the philosophy of consciousness which Schleiermacher so often left in terms of mere implicitness.

The presentation of a structural ontology of immediate self-consciousness (or feeling, or existence), is clearly possible only as a theoretical extrapolation from the specificity of existentially known moments of actual self-consciousness. Actual self-consciousness, as has been indicated, stands as the forefront and focus of the complex arena of consciousness, and reveals in its own formal composition the implicit and potential nature of the two substantive conscious elements: world-consciousness and God-consciousness. But Schleiermacher's insistence that such ontological postulation must be carried out inductively and retrospectively does not lessen his conviction that such theoretical construction is indeed applicable in a universal way to all human self-consciousness. He affirms "the general coherence always postulated in every human consciousness"[2] and finds it to be constituted by "the elements of consciousness,"[3] which are "fundamental"[4] aspects found alike in every human being. These constitutive elements of immediate self-consciousness—world-consciousness, God-consciousness, and actual self-consciousness—are so indubitably fundamental that at one point he even hypostasizes such high abstractions, and calls them facts (*Tatsachen*)[5], portraying them as standing in a constant and definite arrangement with one another.

This ontological "structure" of self-consciousness is supposed by Schleiermacher to be given to every self the same, and it is only in the momentary (ontic) instantiations of individualized existence that the structural elements interact and subject one another to change and confusion. But at their foundational level of existence, the structural elements are "principles of progressive development,"[6] and represent the self's original endowment which can never be substantively changed. The ontological (*existenzial*) "whatness" of the self's consciousness will always remain in its triadic structural form, with the two determining potentialities feeding into the actuality. In contrast, the ontic (*existenziell*) "howness" of self-consciousness will evince the shifting patterns of the actualization of one or

---

[2]Friedrich Schleiermacher, *The Christian Faith*, H.R. Mackintosh and J.S. Stewart, trans. (Edinburgh: T. & T. Clark, 1928), #30,1. Most quotations in English are taken from this translation; where a departure occurs, the translation is my own, taken from the edition of *Der Christliche Glaube* published in 1960 in Berlin by Walter de Gruyter & Co.

[3]Ibid., #71,3.

[4]Ibid., #33,2.

[5]Ibid., #29,1.

[6]Ibid., #66,2.

another potential in dominance over the other. The given structure of existence is constituted as two potential sources of consciousness feeding into one focus of conscious actualization. Consequently, only two of the three given elements are potentials in the sense of bare possibility, while the third is always given as the synthetic state of concrete actualization of the potentiating two.

It is clear, therefore, that the definitiveness of formal actualization is as intrinsic a part of the ontology of existence as are the more substantive potentiating elements of God-consciousness and world-consciousness. Because a complete "actuality" of consciousness is thus founded within the very structure of existence, Schleiermacher demonstrates, as Heidegger and Bultmann do not, that structural ontology is more than simply a theoretical presupposition to the description of the full reality of actual existential moments. Rather, Schleiermacher suggests that both possibility *and* actuality are aspects of the fundamental structure of existence, and that for presuppositional philosophical purposes both must be acknowledged without undue emphasis on either.

In a parallel way Schleiermacher is able to make the same point for theology, suggesting that the locus in consciousness for theological analysis should include not only actual moments of religious existence, but also the potential sources of determination which therein have moved from possibility to actuality. The hermeneutical circle formed by philosophy and theology thus need not be skewed toward either the possibilities or the actuality of existence, but may indeed find itself forming in close symmetry around the entire ground of self-conscious existence, with its fundamental constitution of potentialities and actuality. The living evidence of these structured elements, however, can only be realized fully by the mutual informativeness of philosophy and theology, as the presuppositional implicitness of philosophy is specified and exemplified by the concrete explicitness of theology.

The basic hermeneutical question of criterion, or starting point, is clearly faced by Schleiermacher, even though his critics have often seemed too preoccupied by the theological adequacy of his "pious self-consciousness" to recognize that he ultimately holds this concept as a regulative criterion both for theology and for philosophy, especially his philosophy of self-consciousness. Even though the state of actualized self-consciousness that piety represents—the dominant potentiating of God-consciousness over world-consciousness into actuality—is existentially and historically specific, Schleiermacher still recognizes this as the dominant actualizing of a potential-type element from the general structure of self-consciousness. Even though the God-consciousness is understood *theologically*, in its conjoint but dominant actualizing with world-consciousness, as being a qualitatively unique potential, it still is seen *philosophically* as a constitutive potential of the general structure of self-consciousness.

Even as qualitatively different (in the essential *source* of its potentiation), God-consciousness is present as a fundamental element in the structural constitution of the general self-consciousness. When acknowledged for what it is, therefore, in actual moments of pious feeling related to the world, God-consciousness thereby becomes the ultimate criterion for both theology *and* philosophy. As the finally manifest starting point for the philosophical ontology of self-hood, however, pious actual feeling reveals the fundamental God-consciousness as having been previously obscured and inaccessible, and therefore as fully discernible for philosophy only in a post-suppositional way.

The implications of the theological insight into pious consciousness for philosophical understandings of the nature of consciousness in general are suggested by Schleiermacher in the section of *The Christian Faith* in which he deals with philosophy of religion. Here he points out that only reflection carried out in a state of actual piety (which is the definition of theology) can fully ascertain the God-consciousness as qualitatively different from, or absolutely other than, the world-consciousness. He points out that all other analytical attempts to gauge the true constituents of consciousness are necessarily confused by the sinful outlook of an un-pious person, who tries philosophically to discern that very element of consciousness which that person's state of dominant worldly self-consciousness has obscured. In such an outlook, therefore,

It is possible to give a non-religious explanation of this sense of absolute dependence; it might be said that it only means the dependence of finite particulars on the whole and on the system of all finite things, and that what is implied and made the center of reference is not God but the world.[7]

Before philosophy is informed by the deeper and fuller insights of theology, it interprets the elemental stirrings (*Erregungen*)[8] of the human God-consciousness as simply quantitative intuitions of a unity among the perceptions of world-consciousness. In explicitly designating such a position as pantheistic[9] and flatly immanental, if allowed to extend into theology, Schleiermacher is saying that it belongs instead to an irreligious type of philosophy. Schleiermacher does recognize, however, that in the ontological analyses of his earlier, more philosophical works, such as the *Speeches* and the *Dialectic*, he followed such philosophical argumentation to its own self-delimiting sort of pantheistic conclusion. But he points out in his later theological work that such philosophizing is definitely insufficient to ascertain the full dimensionality of the transcendental reference of the feeling of absolute dependence, and that it can be recognized truly as God-consciousness only in the culminative life-stage of actual piety, or redemption. Schleiermacher therefore upholds the principle *credo ut intelligam* by recognizing that philosophy *per se* cannot ascertain a true philosophy of existence, for without being informed by experiences of dominantly religious existence, philosophy cannot understand the complete structure of existence of which the religious consciousness is a componental part.

---

[7]Ibid., #32,2.

[8]Ibid., #107,1.

[9]Ibid., #32,2 & #46,2.

The Ontological Status of Immediate Self-Consciousness

Setting aside until later the specifically theological consideration of the coursing moments of concretely actualized self-consciousness, our task for now is to focus upon the elemental formation of that consciousness in the fashion of ontologically philosophical considerations of the given nature and status of immediate self-consciousness. Having surveyed the two types of analytical treatment that may be applied to immediate self-consciousness (or human existence, or feeling), we now will use the philosophical type of treatment to discuss exactly what may be the status or locus of this existence. Existence, or immediate self-consciousness for Schleiermacher, will thereby be seen as a certain *level* or locus of human being, and it will be compared in ontological terms with the other, more essential, self-identity level of human being, and also with the larger arena of non-human being. Speaking thus ontologically about existence will of course be recognized as an effort to give a theoretical framework for the later, more phenomenologically, or existentially, rendered description of the actual moments and eventualities of existence. In keeping, however, with Schleiermacher's usual procedure, we will initially spell out in generic ontological terms the framework of human being into which existence falls, as a theoretical basis for the later theological examination of the actual process of existence.

The structure of immediate self-consciousness, or existence, has already been delineated as the potentialities of God-consciousness and world-consciousness conjointly ingressing into the actual self-consciousness. This entire structure of conscious *existence*, however, must now be seen as the superstructural overlay of a substructural level of human being, or what Schleiermacher terms the locus of *essential* self-identity. Immediate self-consciousness is thus categorized by Schleiermacher not as an ephemeral or vapid excrescence, but rather as a really and fully subsisting level of being, ontologically tied to the metaphysically real self of essential human being. Immediate self-consciousness, or existence-as-feeling, is a reproduction or representation of the self's identity at a level of process rather than of stasis. To "exist" as self-conscious means that the person both stands in one's being, as one's position of determination, and stands out of one's being, in one's positing of self-determination. Self-conscious existence is often designated by Schleiermacher as *Dasein*,[10] the peculiarly human form of "being there," as it is by many subsequent existentialist thinkers—but for Schleiermacher there is more essentially determined content in selfhood, with the emphasis on the "being" that is expressed in the "there" of self-consciousness.

The essential substratal being of the individual self, or the *Eigenthümlichkeit*,[11] is the ultimate unity of the self, but even in its unity Schleiermacher supposes it like all other finite beings to have a bipolar constitution. The bipolarity is the mutual coinherence of the ideal and the real indicated in all beings and is seen as the coinherence of soul and body[12] in the human being itself. As an embodied soul, or a conscious being, the essential self finds expression in the extraverting level of "existence," but only as manifesting the two essential and real determinations of its unique (*eigentlich*) identity. These essential and irreducible determinations are derived from God and world, and it is as the two originative sources presented to the determined self that they also are re-presented in immediate self-consciousness. The question of whether there is some sort of correlation between the self's two intrinsic aspects of soul and body and its two extrinsic sources of determination, God and world, is answered by Schleiermacher's peculiar doctrine of dialectic, that is, his concept of bipolar

---

[10] Ibid., #32,1.

[11] Schleiermacher, *Sämmtliche Werke*, III/6, *Psychologie* (Berlin: G. Reimer, 1862) 9. See also *Ethik* in *Schleiermachers Werke*, II, Braun & Bauer, eds. (Leipzig, 1913) 13 & 95.

[12] Ibid., 6-8. In the theoretical introduction to his *Psychologie*, Schleiermacher pursues his ontological analysis of the self to quite metaphysical bases, designating the body-soul polarity of the self as representing the human being's place in the overall ideal-real constitution of being. The *Eigenthümlichkeit* is the same as the *Ich*, and is "the identity of body and soul." The same deduction of a theory of the self is made in the *Ethik* in what Schleiermacher acknowledges is a dialectical manner (248). Yet even in these purely theoretical ontological formulations, Schleiermacher is still anxious to emphasize that these formulae are "descriptively" applicable to empirically-derived knowledge of the soul-body self.

mutual coinherence.¹³ The implication he draws is that God is not *just* the source of soul, nor world *just* the source of body. Rather, the coinhering soul-body unity of essential selfhood has on each side distinctive determinations by God and by world, and these are to be recognized also at the existential level of selfhood, in the actualizing self-consciousness that constitutes itself by the conjoint interaction of God-consciousness and world-consciousness.[14]

Schleiermacher's view that the existing, or feeling, self is an explicit reproduction of the essential self, of which it is "immediately self-conscious," is capsulized in his statement that feeling "is the universal form of the self's having itself."[15] The ontological relation of the two levels of selfhood is clearly that of substantive continuity, and it is for this reason that the dually posited determinations by world and God of the essential self are fully manifested as the dually determinative potentials presented for actualization in the existential self. The crucial difference between the two levels, however, lies in the *manner* of the determinativeness, first by the metaphysical realities of God and world for the essential self, and secondly by the immediately self-conscious representations of God-determination and world-determination for the existing self. The essential self, or *Eigenthümlichkeit*, is postulated by ontological analysis as being a perfectly unified actuality[16] of ideal-real being, so actualized, first, by God, and, secondly, by the world, as its proportionately absolute and relative determinants.

The existing-feeling self is seen, however, to be not only substantively determined by the potential sources of God-consciousness and world-consciousness, but also to be formally affected by its own process of self-actualization. The

---

[13]Schleiermacher, *Dialektik*, L. Jonas, ed., *Sämmtliche Werke*, III/4/II (Berlin: G. Reimer, 1839) 508.

[14]I am indebted for much of this analysis of the constitution of the self in Schleiermacher's thought to the illuminating section on this topic by Richard R. Niebuhr in *Schleiermacher on Christ and Religion* (New York: Scribner's, 1964) 116ff.

[15]Schleiermacher, *Dialektik*, R. Odebrecht, ed. (Leipzig: Hinrichs, 1942) 288.

[16]Schleiermacher, *The Christian Faith*, #94,3.

formal conjoining of the two determinations is intrinsic at the original, essential level of selfhood, but the process of *how* they are to be joined at the *feeling* level involves the mysterious working of human freedom, which is irrefutably granted through the essential self to the existing self. The primal essential self finds itself as completely *posited* in a pattern of being that is ontologically definitive. But it is further posited to "have itself" in the self-actualizing disposition of existence, in which its own *positing* of the two constituent determinations may or may not precisely reduplicate the original pattern. Richard R. Niebuhr says that for Schleiermacher

> the constitution of the self is such that it is capable either of reproducing afresh in itself the true order of these relations, or of distorting that order and thereby denying the structure of being in and through which it lives.[17]

The "structure of being" is the primal and perduring foundation of each living self, the essential selfhood given uniquely to each individual, but so structured that all have it alike in its fundamental elements. The *Ich* of selfhood, moreover, finds itself "posited as positing," or graduating itself into the more expressive level of existential being, that is self-consciousness. Yet it is always the same self which underlies and perdures through all expressions of self-consciousness, that is, "an ego that is the same in all consecutive moments of its existence."[18] In another place Schleiermacher calls the ego "the unity (that) is the essence (*Wesen*) of the subject itself, which manifests itself in these severally distinct forms."[19]

The crucial point, however, is that the essential self is encountered, or at least adumbrated, only in its "self-positing" manifestations in the existing self, and

---

[17]Niebuhr, *Schleiermacher on Christ and Religion*, 198.

[18]Schleiermacher, *The Christian Faith*, #96,1.

[19]Schleiermacher, Ibid., #3,3.

the existing self may or may not perfectly actualize the structure of being already posited at the essential level. God and world are found both hypothetically and empirically to be the basic metaphysical determinants of the self. These assumptions are made, however, only by the self-consciousness, which is immediately conscious of these determinants in their representational forms of God-consciousness and world-consciousness. They *are* the real outside (*äussere*) determinants of the essential self, which is the soul-body self, or knowing-being self, but Schleiermacher must acknowledge that they enter into the existing self only in the imperfect form of potentiating determinations, and thereby are subjected to misrepresentation and even disjunction.

The existing self of feeling, or immediate self-consciousness, thereby is posited at its own level of reality with an implicit ontological structure, which *in ovo* is a precise representation of the essential structure of selfhood underlying it. The primal determinants of God and world are now manifested as God-consciousness and world-consciousness, and they now are found not as intractably proportioned causes of the self, but as malleably interacting potencies for the self-actualizing consciousness. The determinative constituents of the existing self are therefore derived from those of the *essential* self, but now the fundamental "whatness" of their ingression is presented in a new structure of "howness," which is the granted freedom of self-actualization in immediate self-consciousness.

The self-in-feeling thus expresses the determinative *content* of what is given to it, that is, the two potentials, but the *form* in which it expresses them allows it the variability that comes to be known as freedom. The ontological structure of the existing-feeling self is posited for every individual in the same general way, as an actualizing center receiving inputs from two potential determinants, but the way in which the self-actualization proceeds involves every self in its unique life-process of individuation. It is clear, therefore, that for Schleiermacher the self-conscious, existing subject is neither utterly free nor utterly determined; rather, the terms "freedom" and "determination" have different meanings in reference to one or the other of the levels of the self's reality.

The "feeling," by which Schleiermacher designates the process of self-conscious existence, is neither an autonomous capacity for self-creation, nor an *Anknüpfungspunkt* by which a person is directly opened to metaphysical determinations. Rather, feeling suggests the human being's position as intermediate between absolute determination and relative freedom, because one can in existence have experiences or phenomenal indications of both at the same time. Although the person perceives that somehow the essential structure of all being is absolutely determined and given in the very foundation of one's own self-identity, yet the person also perceives that his or her peculiar position of having to re-duplicate this structure allows one in a relative, existential sense to be more or less determined by it. The *how* of one's feeling, of one's actualizing self-consciousness, indicates the further unavoidable positedness of having continuously to become oneself, of necessarily having to choose for oneself new forms of interaction between the two potentiating determinations always presented to one.

The ontological structure of the self's existence is basically a reduplication of the structure of the self's essence, except that the existent self is posited as self-actualizing, rather than as being actualized from without. This central mystery of the freedom in existence is reckoned by Schleiermacher, however, neither to abrogate nor to transcend the simpler level of the essential self underlying it. On the contrary, Schleiermacher is thoroughly convinced that there is no real discontinuity between the two levels of being, and that existence need not be annulled or transmuted in order to partake of the same degree of being as that found in the perfectly actualized determinateness of the essential self. Rather, the human being is a multi-levelled creature, whose uniqueness lies in the ways in which one must make oneself expressive of the essential determinations of one's being. What the person *does* in the movements of self-actualization, however, can be no less real than the determinations infusing them, but certainly no more real than the realities of being and knowing that they represent. If the self is a real polarity of soul and body, or of knowing and being, then this determined polarity of the essential self must be what is determined as expressed further in the existing self, and existence is seen to partake of the same kind of reality as essence, albeit at a different level.[20]

The two outside realities that are determinants of the self, world and God, both give themselves to the constitution of the self through the coinhering modes of being and knowing. The self's essential reality is indeed its being-knowing type of relationship with both world and God: what it is, quite simply, is an entity that can be with and can know both God and world. The self, however, is essentially distinct from its two sources of determination, and finds itself somehow as a subject related through its being-knowing to their distinctly separate metaphysical realities. Whether or not this relationship of the self to its determining "others" is to be termed a "subject-object" relationship depends upon our understanding of Schleiermacher's use of these terms, and certainly he does in many instances want to emphasize the "otherness" or "beyondness" of the self's two sources of determination. And yet, because the knowing-being mode of determination transcends the objective sense of spatio-temporal causation, he also emphasizes the inter-subjective sense of relational causation.

The same mode of knowing-being determination that characterizes the relational subsistence of the essential self naturally obtains also at the level of the existing self. The immediate self-consciousness, or feeling, or existence, is constituted also as a knowing-being relationship to both sources of determination, only now at the level of reduplication and personal actualization of the constituent influences. The indeterminate *manner* of the self-conscious actualization in feeling, therefore, does not mean that the original sources of determination are now less real in the realm of existence. To the contrary, even though they are now termed "potentials," the determinative constituents still are the only material contents available to be actualized in self-existence, and the existing self still relates to them in the essentially given fashion of knowing and being. The most self-expressive degree of existence is still directly or immediately related to its ingredient

---

[20]Ibid., #34,1.

elements of outside determination, and the feeling-of-existence is found to be still the knowing-being type of relationship to the originative elements. Feeling is the self's actualization or "re-having" of its intrinsic constitution: it is the self's immediate consciousness not just of the self *a se*, but of the self-as-determined by outside constituents. Feeling is thus the self's knowing and being, not just of and with itself, but of and with the outside others which are posited to it as the basic constituents of reality.

The elemental structure of existence—the two potentiating determinants and their joint actualization—is seen by Schleiermacher as an ontological model of the complex but synthetic life of the self, and as such to be a direct outcropping of the underlying givenness of the essential self. Every reflective attempt to deduce or to describe the general nature of the self is recognized by Schleiermacher as inadequate, at least in comparison with the specific, phenomenal expressions of the self that he says must be the beginning of any philosophical or theological discussion. The *actual moments* of self-consciousness, which in ontological nature are the conjoint presentations of the self's determinations by God and world, are seen as the only real "points of entry" into the hermeneutical circle which aims to connect self-consciousness with its real sources of determination.

> If we compare these three possible forms [God-consciousness, world-consciousness, and actual self-consciousness] with each other, it is clear that descriptions of human states of mind with this content can only be taken from the realm of inner experience, and that therefore in this form nothing alien can creep into the system of Christian doctrine.[21]

The "inner experience" that Schleiermacher refers to is the immediate self-consciousness, and when taken with its full content of reference to the whole of encompassing reality, it is seen as the most original and only valid ontic content

---

[21]Ibid., #30,2.

for ontological analyses. Bearing in mind that the ontologically conceptualized *structure* of self-consciousness is presented by Schleiermacher only as a presuppositional framework for the theologically explicit presentation of the *process* of actual moments of that self-consciousness, we will set our first task as the explication of that structure in its triadic form of world-consciousness, God-consciousness, and actual self-consciousness. In this structural setting we shall see how the potency-actuality thrust of processing consciousness occurs, and the two potencies of God-consciousness and world-consciousness will be seen at the existential level as unavoidably disproportionate competitors for domination of the living moments of actual self-consciousness.

WORLD-CONSCIOUSNESS

The Strength of Influence by the World-Consciousness

Although the three structural elements of immediate self-consciousness are given *in loco* at the beginning of life, the sensible self-consciousness, or world-consciousness, is usually examined first by Schleiermacher because of its rapid developmental potential in every human history. The basic reason for its historical precedence, although not its ontological precedence, will naturally be further examined as the crux of the origin of sin, as the early dominance of world-consciousness over God-consciousness.

For the present line of ontological analysis, however, it must suffice to say that the ontological status of the sensible self-consciousness is characterized by its direct and multifarious openness to the real world of finite being, which is its given source of determination. World-consciousness is the consciousness of the self's determination by the world, a world that the self can discern as ontologically similar to its own constitution as coinherently real-ideal being. Not only is the world at large perceived as a real-ideal polarity, but every individual being as well is perceived as being like the individual self in having a material and a formal aspect.[22]

The means by which the self becomes conscious of the analogous constitution of other worldly beings is through its objective level of consciousness, or perception (*Wahrnehmung*), or intuition (*Anschauung*).[23] The outer-directed objective consciousness is the functional extension of the inner-based world-consciousness, for the objectifying functions of thinking and willing are mediating extensions of the inner-feeling type thought and will that compose the inner world-consciousness. Sensible feeling, or world-consciousness, realizes that its bipolar aspects of receptivity and activity (its ontological knowing and being) are actually connected to the outside world through another mediating level of consciousness, that is, the objectifying functions of thinking and willing. The inner world-consciousness is so quickly and widely activated, therefore, because the sense impressions occasioning it are present as soon as the objective consciousness of intellection and perception connects or mediates the outside world to the inside life of feeling. The world-consciousness, or world-feeling, is not the same as the impressing sense data themselves but is the whole panoply of immediately self-conscious feelings that the mediating data occasion. In this way, the world-consciousness remains firmly situated in the structure of immediate self-consciousness, for it is the consciousness of the self as it is determined *via* thinking and willing by the other ideal-real beings of the world. It involves every feeling of dependence upon a determining other that can be sensibly perceived by means of the objectively oriented intellect and will.

---

[22]Schleiermacher, *Dialektik*, (Jonas) 393-94.

[23]Schleiermacher early tried to clarify the difference between feeling (*Gefühl*) and intuition (*Anschauung*), in response to the initial confusion created by the *Speeches*. In trying to give *Anschauung* more objective reference to the sensible world, he compares it to perception (*Wahrnehmung*) in the *Dialektik* (Jonas, 61-62). By the time of *The Christian Faith*, he uses *Anschauung* and *Wahrnehmung* as virtually interchangeable terms to designate the functioning of the objective consciousness (*gegenständliches Bewusstsein*) (#5,1).

World-Consciousness as Receptive and Active in Its Knowing and Being towards the World

The sensible self-consciousness receives its most succinct definition by Schleiermacher as

> the self-consciousness which, as expressing the connection [*via* thinking and willing] with perceptible finite being, splits up into a partial feeling of dependence and a partial feeling of freedom.[24]

The connection (*Beziehung*) between my being and the rest of finite being is that which is mediated by the "objective" modes of thinking and willing. The "subjective" self-consciousness that looks upon this sensible determination of the self and expresses (*ausdrückt*) it as a feeling about being so determined is the sensible self-consciousness. The self's feeling about being dependent upon these worldly determinations is also bipolar and is expressed in its bipolar modes of inner thought and will as "a partial feeling of dependence and a partial feeling of freedom." The dependence and the freedom as sensible feelings of the self's relation to the world are thus basically equivalent to the sensible feelings of thought and will as the self's relation to the world. The thought-feeling, as more of a dependence, or receptivity from the world, is seen as coinherently operative with the will-feeling, as more of a freedom or activity toward the world. Thought-receptivity is indeed completely coinherent with will-activity in the bipolar world-consciousness, for any sensibly derived feeling that one is being affected *by* another must, in this dialectical form of existence, redound to a reciprocal channeling of affective activity back towards that other.

While "coinherence"[25] is the pattern of the self's two aspects as being together *within* self-consciousness, the pattern of "reciprocity" is the manner of

---

[24] Schleiermacher, *The Christian Faith*, #5,1.

[25] "*Ineinandersein*," Braun & Bauer, II, *Ethik*, 248.

that integrated self's conscious relationship *to* the outside "other" beings in the world. Reciprocity, or *Wechselwirkung*,[26] is a "working in alternation" of one being upon another, with the emphasis upon their objective ontological distinction from one another—even though they do have "affective" impact upon one another at the level of each one's inner self-consciousness. The given self, and the many other selves and beings of the world, are so constituted that they may affectively receive and offer (within their real, inner coinherence of thought-being, or receptivity-activity) impacts upon one another, albeit through the reciprocally transmitting medium of the objective consciousness. The two patterns of ontological dialectic that Schleiermacher sees throughout all of finite being thus are characterized as a "coinherence" (of ideal and real, or thought and will) *within* every being, and as a "reciprocity" of objectively transmitted intersubjectivity *among* all beings.

Reciprocity between Self and World in the Sensible Self-Consciousness

Schleiermacher thinks of the *coinhering* dependence and freedom *within* the sensible self-consciousness "as of one" (*als Eines*), and in this way the self affectively disposes itself as an entity in regard to a reciprocating other.

> Let us now think of the feeling of dependence and the feeling of freedom as of one, in the sense that not only the subject but the co-posited other is the same for both. Then the total [sensible] self-consciousness made up of both together is one of reciprocity between the subject and the co-posited other. Now let us suppose the totality of all moments of feeling, of both kinds as one whole: then the co-posited other is also to be supposed as a totality, or as one, and then that term "reciprocity" is the right one for our [sensible] self-consciousness in general, inasmuch as it expresses our connection with everything which either appeals to our receptivity or is subjected to our activity. And this is true not only when we particularize this other and ascribe to each of

---

[26]Schleiermacher, *The Christian Faith*, #4,2.

> its elements a different degree of relation to the twofold consciousness within us, but also when we think of the total "outside" as one, and moreover (since it contains other receptivities and activities to which we have a relation) as one together with ourselves, that is, as a *world*.
>
> Accordingly, our self-consciousness, as a consciousness of our being in the world or of our being with the world, is a series in which the feeling of freedom and the feeling of dependence are divided. . . . So that our whole self-consciousness in relation to the world or its individual parts remains enclosed within these limits.[27]

Because the self feels the world as both providing affective input and asking affective engagement in return, it feels the active participation of "being *in* the world," yet also the passive distinctiveness of "being *with* the world." However, in both cases (that is, the integral "coinherence" of activity and receptivity, which then has "reciprocity" with the world), the sensible self-consciousness finds its "two-fold" feeling toward the world as definitely characterized and even circumscribed by the same sphere of knowing and being as the world. Schleiermacher clearly intends to demarcate the finiteness, or relativity, by which the sensible self-consciousness "remains enclosed within these limits," for in being determined by the very knowing and being which constitute the world, the sensible self-consciousness finds itself as characterized also by the same finite limits.

> But neither an absolute feeling of dependence, i.e. without any feeling of freedom in relation to the co-determinant, nor an absolute feeling of freedom, i.e. without any feeling of dependence in relation to the co-determinant, is to be found in this whole realm.[28]

---

[27] Ibid., #4,2.

[28] Ibid.

Sensible Self-Consciousness as the Realm of Antithesis between Self and Another

Indeed, it is due to the feelings of relative freedom and relative dependence which the self shares reciprocally with the other beings of the world that it has a point of departure, though not of comparison, for discerning the utter singularity of that contrasting feeling of dependence which posits self and world as altogether being determined by the absolute other. The realm of sensible self-consciousness itself is thus denominated by Schleiermacher as being the "realm of the particular" (*Gebiet des Vereinzelten*)[29] in its awareness of the separateness of the self from all other worldly beings, and yet of their co-posited (*mitgesetzte*)[30] interrelatedness with one another. This realm of particular existence, as conveying the self by sensible means to the others of the world so as to receive reciprocal confirmation from their particularity, is what is also described as the realm of antithesis (*Gegensatz*), or reciprocity between the self and another:

> The realm of the particular . . . is subject to the antithesis [of self and other] . . . [but] these feelings are most definitely distinguished from the feeling of absolute dependence, [where] all antithesis between one individual and another is done away. Hence there seems to be no objection to our distinguishing three levels [*Stufen*] of self consciousness: The confused animal level, in which the antithesis cannot arise, as the lowest; the sensible self-consciousness, which rests entirely upon the antithesis, as the middle; and the feeling of absolute dependence, in which the antithesis again disappears and the subject unites and identifies itself with everything which, in the middle level, was set over against it, as the highest.[31]

---

[29]Ibid., #5,1.

[30]Ibid., #4,2.

[31]Ibid., #5,1.

The basic distinction that Schleiermacher is making here is a qualitative one, which clearly indicates a real difference between the realm of relative dependence and the realm of absolute dependence. While both realms are indeed reckoned as of the same genre *qua* self-consciousness—that is, as the two potentiating powers of self-conscious feeling—they are also found to have qualitatively different sources, which are the two underlying determinants of the self, that is, the world and God. Schleiermacher's terming these two structurally equiposed realms as "levels" (*Stufen*) of self-consciousness is rather puzzling at this point, but seems to be pointing equivocally toward two more common descriptive contexts for the realms of self-consciousness.

On the one hand, he ordinarily refers to world-consciousness and God-consciousness in *ontological* terms as similar "components" or "potential elements" of actualizing self-consciousness, with only their sources acknowledged as being typologically different as metaphysical determinants of the underlying self. On the other hand, he often refers to the "stages" through which the actual self-consciousness passes in its historical process of alternating dominance by either God-or world-consciousness. In this context, it is possible to see the term "level" as referring to the historically "lower" stage of sinful *dominance* by world-consciousness, or to the "higher" stage of graceful *dominance* by God-consciousness. In both the ontological and the historical descriptions of self-consciousness, therefore, it is clear that any "gradation" or qualitative comparison of the two components is due not to their structural setting within self-consciousness, but to the contrasting underlying power of their sources of determination.

The Contrast Between World-Consciousness and God-Consciousness

In the final analysis, the realm of the particular, sensible consciousness is set apart from the realm of the absolute-dependence-consciousness because the world of sense involves "feelings" in profuse plurality, while the unitary realm of absoluteness involves only "*the* feeling" of absolute dependence. The multiplicious realm of sensible feelings, deriving from the manifold world of finite being, is found as qualitatively different from the singular realm of one feeling for the infinite, indeed, *because* all particular feelings of dependence and freedom are found as posited in their very relatedness by a unified source of absolute determination. The absolute "positing" can be known as the source of all interrelated "positedness" simply because both realms become determinants of the human self and its intermediate consciousness.

The exact meaning of Schleiermacher's "lowest, animal level of self-consciousness in which the antithesis cannot arise" is best left to conjecture, for Schleiermacher never elaborates this concept as more than a hypothetical ballast in his scheme of gradations. The only ontologically and historically real elements of self-consciousness are the two actually mutually implicative realms of world- and God-consciousness, and it has now been determined that they imply one another not in the sense of coinhering polarity, but in the sense of reciprocally contrasting determinations of the self. The possibility of a pantheistic interpretation of Schleiermacher is disallowed again at this point, for Schleiermacher clearly indicates that the world, even as a manifold unity including all distinct beings, is only a relative and synthetic unity, and as such is still absolutely dependent upon a transcendent ground of determination.

Schleiermacher's statement that "the feeling of absolute dependence is (where) all antithesis between one individual and another is done away" indicates this as the self's feeling of standing in complete solidarity with all other beings, in together being utterly determined by the absolute. The antithesis among all worldly beings both separates and unites them but is unalterably characteristic of their common state of relativity. The antithesis between finite beings can be "done away" only in the consciousness of a particular being who feels himself and all his other fellow beings as absolutely dependent upon an "other" source for their very being in such co-implicative relativity. When Schleiermacher says that in the feeling of absolute dependence "all antithesis between one individual and another is done away," he is therefore referring to the elimination of barriers between the finite beings who stand before the absolute, and not to any sort of pantheistic elimination of barriers between a finite individual and the absolute other. Any given self who becomes dominantly open to the feeling of absolute dependence is for Schleiermacher by definition made aware of the infinite distinction between oneself and the absolute, and thereby simply finds all relative antithesis between itself and worldly others as "done away." It is in this sense of focusing the self-consciousness upon its absolute determinateness, as its highest potential level or gradation, that the subject is able to "unite and identify itself with everything which, in the middle level, was set over against it."

The Manifold Relativity of World-Consciousness

Even in the highest existential state, of dominant God-consciousness, the world-consciousness is still fully present as the other given component of actual self-consciousness. It continually presents itself as the consciousness that the manifold particularity of the world is "united" with the self, and not "done away" as it would be if God-consciousness were able to exist alone. The "unity" of self and others realized within world-consciousness is necessarily relative, however, for the antithesis of reciprocity between finite beings is endemically given.

> We recognize in our [actual] self-consciousness an awareness of the world, but it is different from the awareness of God in the same self-consciousness. For the world, if we assume it to be a unity, is nevertheless in itself a divided and disjointed unity which is at the same time the totality of all contrasts and differences and of all the resulting manifold determinations, of which every man is one, partaking in all the contrasts.
> To be one with the world in self-consciousness is nothing else than being conscious that we are a living part of this whole; and this cannot possibly be a consciousness of absolute dependence; the more so that all living parts stand in reciprocal interaction with each other.[32]

---

[32]Ibid., #32,2.

It is precisely because of the reciprocal interaction among all living beings, including both dependence and freedom, that their feeling of unity must be one of relativity, that is, of interactive affectation of one another, and cannot entail a feeling simply of absolute dependence. The sensible awareness of the relative unity of the network of created being, or of a "world," is the awareness of a *synthetic* unity, divided and disjointed, composed of "manifold . . . contrasts and differences." Our feeling of dependence upon this world-unity, in contradistinction to pantheism can only be a feeling of relatively unified interaction, including the responding feeling of freedom, and thus could never be a feeling of absolute dependence upon a perfect unity.

Nowhere does Schleiermacher make it clearer as to the absolute transcendence of the divine "one" than in his discussion of its radical distinction from the finite world known to world-consciousness. Even though the absolute somehow gives itself to every finite life of self-consciousness, the process is that of the absolute's revelation of its determination of the entire world of finite being, including the very self and its consciousness. The finite modes of knowing and being, as coinhering in every particular reality of the world, are acknowledged by sensible self-consciousness as the overall constitution of the entire interrelated world; yet the definite positedness of their complex unity indicates that such synthetic reality is absolutely dependent upon a transcendent source beyond itself. God is thereby conceived by Schleiermacher as clearly more than the immanently self-constituting *Aufhebung* of a universal dialectic of worldly components. Neither can God be conceived as the futuristically consequent reconciliation of the polarities of existence. Rather, God-as-absolute is distinctively present as the before-, during-, and after-ground of finite reality, which reality in its utter dependence reflects in all ways as its absolute determination.

The sensible world-consciousness thus involves an overall feeling of the self's systemic unification with all other worldly being. This sense of being "altogether" is that of an utterly (*schlecthinnig*) dependent and limited process, utterly contingent upon a transcendent positing of all its continuous relativity as a world.

The sensible self-consciousness, of the self with its world, is for Schleiermacher clearly distinct, both in content and in form, from the God-consciousness, which meets it in the common arena of actual self-consciousness. Yet for all their ontological separateness, the two realms of consciousness determination do become reciprocally related within the existential forum of actual moments of self-consciousness. In a philosophically paradoxical conclusion of the problem of the many and the one, the existential setting of self-consciousness places the many of the world in disproportionate juxtaposition to the absolute one. The juxtaposition does occur as the given conjunctive process of existing self-actualization, but only because the "many" of the world seem constitutionally driven to find a relative systemic unity, and thereby to pose the question of an absolute unity, which can only be transcendentally answered.

The contention that both the multifaceted question of finite being and its conclusive single answer can be conjointly ascertained within the context of self-consciousness is certainly Schleiermacher's central theological conundrum, but it is the *coup de résistance* of his theology as well. The positing of existential questing toward the determined limits of finite being is reckoned by Schleiermacher as the ultimate pose of worldly self-consciousness, and is found to be answerable only by a revelation posited also within self-consciousness, but one which absolutely transcends the question in the process.

The very givenness of finite being in its questioning pose portrays the insight of natural theology that manifold being has an inner drive for unity, which is a thrust toward the opening, widening, and finally the fulfilling of the given limitations. The insight of revealed theology, in conjunction if not in correlation, is that these non-self-derived strivings for unity within finite being are derived, sustained, and fulfilled by an absolute source of all gratuitous determination. The limiting questions of natural world-consciousness, presented by both moral feelings and thought feelings, seem to suggest, but not to presuppose, an answer not in that kind, but in a transcendingly absolute mode. In Wittgenstein's phrase, so also for Schleiermacher, "not how the world is, is the mystical, but that it is."[33]

The Actual Precedence of World-Consciousness

The question of why the worldly self-consciousness takes procedural precedence over the God-consciousness may now be seen as more than simply a logical issue. Rather, the procedural order of appearance of world-consciousness, both in life and in logic, takes on for Schleiermacher the further significance of ontological and existential ordering. It is clear that the world-consciousness has an equal *structural* footing with God-consciousness in the fundamental make-up of the actual self-consciousness, yet it is also clear that in the *process* of development of actual conscious life, the world-consciousness inevitably succeeds to a preemptive role. Why it is that the consciousness of worldly multiplicity and its polarized interrelationships should initially overcome the consciousness of absolute unity is for Schleiermacher answered only partially by ontological analysis, and also only partially by actual existential analysis. The combination of the two modes of analysis will constitute a philosophical framework for the concept of sin, which then can be informed by the theological insights of predominating piety, to specify the exact relationship of sin to grace.

In our present consideration of the ontological status of world-consciousness *per se*, the only way of explaining its ascendancy over the structurally coeval God-consciousness would seem to be by a substantive elucidation of its manifold and intensely present panoply of sensible feelings, always ready for potentiation into the actual self-consciousness. The reason for the multifarious and intense presence of sensible feelings, giving them a different sort of impetus for potentiating into actuality than that of the feeling of the absolute, is their inherent similarity to the finite self doing the actualizing. The worldly sources of sensible self-consciousness are composed of the same ideal-real, or knowing-being, polarity

---

[33]Ludwig Wittgenstein, *Tractatus Logico-Philosophicus* (London: Kegan Paul, Tranch, Trubner & Co., 1922) 186.

as is the very ideal-real, soul-body self which is expressing its determinative sources in actual self-consciousness.

In expressing the worldly side of its determinations, the sensible feelings so oriented are naturally reflective of the ideal-real or thought-will polarity of all worldly finitude, and therefore portray all worldly things to the actual self-consciousness as having the same ideal-real constitution which it exemplifies. The knowing-being constitution of actual self-consciousness somehow seems *qua* an entity of worldly finitude to be more available to potentiating feelings from the outside finite world, even though it also has the potential for turning its knowing-being selfhood toward the absolute side of its determination. The finite self-consciousness finds itself to be more similar to the knowing-form and being-substance of the worldly sources of its sensible feelings than it does to the unified knowing-being which is simply given to it from an absolute source.

There is in Schleiermacher the clear suggestion that the absoluteness of God's determinative power is shown by a divine ordination that within the plane of human consciousness, world-consciousness will precede God-consciousness, at least in the historical development of actualization, if not in ontological potentiality. God therefore posits humans under this "law of earthly existence that, . . . the sensuous self-consciousness developed first in each individual, while the God-consciousness came only later."[34] The process by which "sensuous consciousness developed first" *seems* to be one of historical contingency, but for Schleiermacher it is as much a part of the divine ordination for humankind as is the ontological prepositioning which would *seem* originally to equilibrate world- and God-consciousness. How it is that the given ontological structure of consciousness can in principle be balanced, yet in developing actuality be weighted first to one side and then to the other, is the conundrum that Schleier-

---

[34]Schleiermacher, *The Christian Faith*, #89,3.

macher says is only seemingly explained by the freedom of human self-actualizing, but in reality is to be explained by the "unity of the divine decree."[35]

The given *structure* of self-consciousness, by which the two pre-determined potentials conjointly constitute the moments of actuality, must be seen as developed by Schleiermacher as a theoretical modelling of an implicit ontology. On the other hand, the developmental *process* of the actualizing consciousness is seen as the true locus of existential reality, as it alternates states of dominance by one or the other potency. While the structure is ordained by God as originative or constitutive, so also is its processing actuality ordained to carry it through varying stages of existential representation. Thus, even though the sensible consciousness is historically experienced as primally assertive, the fundamental power of God-consciousness also is so constantly potentiating that it is typically able to break through into actual conscious dominance at some point in every given human history.

> The God-consciousness came only later, and up to a point gradually took possession of the sensuous self-consciousness and subjugated it.[36]

It is clear that Schleiermacher believes this train of historical development to be the basic destined course of human existence, for he definitely speaks of the God-consciousness in qualitatively superlative terms as the "highest level"[37] of self-consciousness. Because of the already mentioned affinity between the actualizing self's polar identity and the polarity of knowing-being which characterizes the sources of sensible self-consciousness, the sensible feelings are destined to be stronger in the initial stage of life. This, however, is only because the sensible feelings serve as the quantitative *alter ego* to their eventual sublation by the God-consciousness. The process of life is one in which the actualizing self comes to

---

[35]Ibid.

[36]Ibid.

[37]Ibid., #5,1.

realize that its entire panoply of relative feelings toward the world is utterly dependent upon an absolute source of both the world and the self's relative capacity to be related to it. And unlike Heidegger's later program for extending the Schleiermacherian phenomenology of existence in an Husserlian manner, the basic thrust of Schleiermacher's thought is that the sensible *Umwelt* of a person's world-feelings is the *alter ego* not just to an autonomously self-constituting existence, but is the *alter ego* to the absolute power of determination which posits self in between the two realities.

The Predominance of World-Consciousness as Leading to Sin

In anticipation of the more properly theological question of whether sin is derived from within the self, and its conscious life of will and thought, or from without, in the world of sense and matter, the answer can be seen as framed by Schleiermacher in terms of "both-and," rather than "either-or." The self is given in its basic pose of existence as responsible for the actualized feelings it brings into being, but yet it also finds the strengths of its two potential sources of feeling so presented to it that it inevitably chooses the one before the other. Since the one source—world-feelings—is recognized as altogether determined by the other source—feelings of absolute dependence—it is asserted by Schleiermacher that the worldly is allowed initial precedence only because the Godly can subsume and overcome it.

The material world is therefore acknowledged as intrinsically good, as is the sensible range of world-feelings which are consciously disposed towards it. The *possibility* of evil dislocation arises because of the ontologically determined arrangement of conscious existence—given to the self from without. In contrast, the *actuality* of evil as humanly projected sin arises from within, in the self's own capacity for existential actualization of the given structure. As in the view of religious phenomenologist Paul Ricoeur, sin is experienced by a person both as ineluctably forced upon one from without, and as implicitly chosen by the person as one's own voluntary action.[38] Yet in the final reckoning of his theological deliberation, Schleiermacher seems clearly to indicate that the aspect of outside ontological *determination* is the real explanatory principle of both good and evil in a person, for both are found as inevitable outcomes of the divine plan of creation and redemption.

The rather Augustinian certainty of Schleiermacher's inclusion of both good and evil within the purview of absolute divine determination is a reflection also of the Augustinian certainty that absolute will is more to be attributed to the divine than is absolute knowledge, which is only subsidiary to will. The all-determinative will of God ordains the entire reality of creation as good,[39] and therefore also ordains the divisions of world-consciousness from God-consciousness and sin from redemption as simply relative antitheses within the embracement of the ultimate source and end of their finite reality.

The supposition that many have drawn from Schleiermacher's ultimate theological principle is that the absolute creativity, or embracement, of divine determination obviates the reality both of human existence and of its sinful self-assertion. A fuller picture of his theologically complex intentions, however, would indicate that for him human existence as self-actualizing consciousness is indeed real, just *because* it is so posited by the absolute will. In the same sense, the reality of sin as a phenomenon of human actuality is supported by the divine grant of free will, and the divine arrangement of world- and God-consciousness to be potentials for that free will.

Whether sin is found to be ontologically or semantically real for Schleiermacher will of course depend upon the sense we can derive from his principles of absoluteness as pure reality, and relativity as the dialectic of being and knowing. But whatever the soundness of his logic and his semantics, it seems clear that Schleiermacher's intention is to say that sin is a reality of our lives,

---

[38]Paul Ricoeur, *The Symbolism of Evil* (Boston: Beacon Press, 1967).

[39]Schleiermacher, *The Christian Faith*, #55,2.

even though in the divine view it is a relative stage in the absolute process of redemption-effecting-creation.

Consonantly, in the ontological terminology of the structure of human reality, the world-consciousness must be seen in its original potentiating dominance over God-consciousness as only a relative stage in the process of the divine self-presentation to humans, which later is to be reversed in the redemptive stage of dominant God-consciousness. In the consummating stage of human existence, the divine ordination of the human stages is fully revealed. It is then understood that only along with the sensible consciousness, in its worldly capacity to relate to the historical Jesus Christ, can the God-consciousness be capacitated and actualized in the human self, along the same lines as it was perfectly actualized in Jesus.[40]

GOD-CONSCIOUSNESS

God-Consciousness as a Structural Component in the Ontology of Existence

The God-consciousness, or the feeling of absolute dependence, is for Schleiermacher the other constitutive element in the basic structure of self-consciousness, because it potentiates along with world-consciousness into moments of actual self-consciousness. The God-consciousness also involves feelings of the self-as-determined by an "other" beyond the self, but the actual temporal "feelings" are in essence expressions of a single undifferentiated feeling of a single unitary source determining the self, that is, *the* feeling of absolute dependence. The singular feeling of absolute dependence is thus radically different from the multifarious plurality of feelings that in quantity become feelings of relative dependence and relative freedom, or the manifold world-consciousness. Only as *structurally* covalent constituents, or potentials, for actual self-consciousness, therefore, can God-consciousness and world-consciousness be said to be similar.

---

[40]Ibid., #105,1.

It is in the sense of ontological possibility that Schleiermacher wants to certify the God-consciousness, like the world-consciousness, as being a potentiating constituent, or element (*Lebenselement*),[41] of the full life of existing self-consciousness. It is because he assumes this ontological equilibration that Schleiermacher must conceive of both constitutive elements as "presuppositions"[42] or "potentials"[43] underlying the actual self-consciousness. Even though as ontological presuppositions the concept of "elements" or "potentials" may be too hypostasized, Schleiermacher must capture in terms of ontological locus and function the essentially fluid constituents of self-consciousness which are continuously provided by the two sources of the self's determination. Only in this way can he logically refer to these phylogenetic existential principles as universal elements found in every human nature, and this he does, first with world-consciousness, and secondly with God-consciousness.

> This feeling of absolute dependence, in which our self-consciousness represents the finitude in general of our being, is therefore not an accidental element, or a thing which varies from person to person, but is a universal element of life.[44]

We may first note here that the "feeling of absolute dependence" is designated as an element of every human life, but more importantly we must note that the reason for its universality is its presence as that mode of consciousness which manifests the complete connectedness of all things under one universal source of absolute metaphysical determination. This elemental feeling is so singular because it "re-presents" (*vertritt*) into consciousness the singular truth that

---

[41]Ibid., #33, int.

[42]Ibid., #32, int.

[43]Ibid., #66,2 & #93,2.

[44]Ibid., #33, int.

our being is joined with all others (finitude in general) under the utter determination of an absolute source.

> That the feeling of absolute dependence as such is the same in all, and not different in different persons, follows from the fact that it does not rest upon any particular modification of human existence (*Dasein*), but upon the absolutely general being (*Wesen*) of man, which contains in itself the potentiality of all those differences by which the particular content of the individual personality is determined.[45]

The God-consciousness is presupposed as an ontologically given element in all men because it *cannot* be explained by any of the multifarious particularized instances of *Dasein* (actual self-consciousness). It must rather be reckoned as *the* universally singular determination of the person's essential being (*Wesen*) as such, that is only "re-presented" into the actual process of self-consciousness as the feeling of absolute dependence.

Even though the absolute determinant is the essential source of both the self and its reciprocally-determining world, yet at the level of existence, or immediate self-consciousness, it is ontogenetically re-presented as but one of two co-eval elements of the self's existence. And when *in medias res* of actual moments of conjoined consciousness, it is difficult upon reflection to distinguish the world-conscious element from the God-conscious element, Schleiermacher still insists that the distinction is not simply made for theoretical ontological neatness, but that it is derived ultimately from the two radically distinct sources of the essential self's determination. The God-consciousness is called a datum (*Tatsache*) of the self-consciousness in the very sense that it remains the same—as an ontological element—in all the dialectical combinations to which it is subjected at the actualizing level of consciousness.[46]

---

[45]Ibid., #33,1.

[46]Ibid., #29,1.

The kind of ontological status which obtains for this elemental "datum" of consciousness is therefore somehow in between the metaphysical reality of the *essential* self as absolutely determined and the representational reality of the *existing* self-consciousness. That ontological status, as has already been seen in regard to the world-consciousness, is the status of a "potential," or a "capacity" (*Fähigkeit*)[47] for representing the essential reality of the self's absolute determination into the overt level of actualized self-conscious reality.

In the status of a potential, moreover, the God-consciousness is not tinged by unreality, but rather, in the Aristotelian sense, it is the ever present power or potency for conscious existential actualization of the *essential* determination underlying it. Schleiermacher thus speaks of "the potency (*Kräftigkeit*) of the God-consciousness to give the impulse to all life's [actually self-conscious] moments,"[48] which is ontologically present even though not always existentially dominant. In its purely theological language, the redeemed self will finally recognize this potency as having been "the spirit's demand . . . always the same,"[49] even though as a potentiating force (*Grösse*) it has always been subject to the vagaries of the freely existing human consciousness.

The Qualitative Difference of God-Consciousness from World-Consciousness in Reference to Source

However much Schleiermacher emphasizes the similarity of God-consciousness and world-consciousness in human ontological status, as potentiating components of conscious existence, it is nonetheless clear that he regards them as qualitatively distinct in regard to their ultimate metaphysical origins. The God-consciousness is clearly derived from the "higher" and "absolute" source of all metaphysical determination, which source is thus transcendent and determin-

---

[47]Ibid.

[48]Ibid., #93,2.

[49]Ibid., #67,2.

ative of both humankind and the world. To say that God, or the absolute, is metaphysically prior to humankind and to the world is also to imply that in the order of a person's conscious recapitulation of one's determinations, the level of consciousness of unitary absoluteness is prior to and inclusive of the consciousness of worldly multiplicity. The God-consciousness is derived from neither the world nor the self: it simply potentiates within the self-consciousness to explicate the self's and the world's absolute determinateness. The God-consciousness is posited as the highest form of consciousness because "here no causal agency can be attributed to the person who is being taken up into fellowship, for the higher form cannot be in any way derived from the lower stages of life."[50]

The "higher" form of consciousness is designated as such because through it the self perceives that its entire essential being is absolutely determined, and this consciousness thus becomes the self's actual reception and acknowledgement of its underlying determinative source. The absolute source determines within the self's level of conscious feeling "the consciousness of being absolutely dependent, or which is the same thing [in theological retrospect] of being in relation with God."[51] In order for this feeling of dependence upon the absolute to occur as a form of immediate *self*-consciousness, it must nonetheless be understood as a co-positing, *at the level of existence-consciousness*, of the self with the absolute, even as it points to the underlying determinative distinction *in essence* between them.

> The *Whence* of our receptive and active existence [*Dasein*], as coposited [*mitgesetzte*] in this self-consciousness, is to be designated by the word "God". . . . God signifies for us simply that which is the co-determinant [*das Mitbestimmende*] in this feeling, and to which [*worauf*] we trace our being [*Sosein*] in such a state.[52]

---

[50]Ibid., #108,6.

[51]Ibid., #4, int.

[52]Ibid., #4,4

A person's deepest existential feeling is for Schleiermacher that which conveys to one immediately the true depth of one's essential origin. In both the (existential) feeling of absolute dependence and the (essential) underlying metaphysical reality of the self's absolute determinateness, the absolute is found to be in direct and fundamental control: "Along with the absolute dependence which characterizes not only man but all finite being [*endliches Sein*], there is given to man also the immediate self-consciousness of it, which becomes a consciousness of God."[53]

God is the source of *all* being, both the self's essential being and its existential being-as-consciousness. As source and determinant of all, he is as much determinative of the "existential" self-in-consciousness as he is of the "essential" self beneath consciousness. This is why Schleiermacher is so adamant in maintaining that the objectively real God can and must be present in the subjectively real domain of human-being-as-conscious existent. This utter pervasiveness of the absolute at all levels of dependent reality is why Schleiermacher sees no logical confusion, therefore, in postulating the "presence of God" within human self-consciousness. Because human self-consciousness, or feeling, is one of the domains of reality—that is the most actually real aspect of human being—it is only natural that the absolute determinant of all reality be present to it: "God is given [*gegeben*] to us in feeling in an original way."[54]

God-Consciousness as Maintaining Self and World as Totally Different from God

The close connection between the divine and the human within self-consciousness is thus understood by Schleiermacher as revealing the determinative connection that is indicated in the whole of being itself. Nevertheless, he would find many interpreters who discerned either pantheism or psychologism in his emphasis on human feeling as a locus of divine self-giving. This theme certainly was suggested in many of his early writings, and could be inferred even from his

---

[53]Ibid.

[54]Ibid.

less "romantic" later theological writings, where he sometimes continued the use of language suggestive of such ontologistic positions.

> The immediate feeling of absolute dependence is presupposed and contained in every Christian religious self-consciousness as the only way in which, in general, our own being and the infinite being of God can be one (*Eines*) in self-consciousness.[55]

The thrust of most other statements, however, both theological and philosophical, is unequivocal in maintaining that a person's contact with God within consciousness is the simple, or "absolute" (*schlechthinnig*), dispensation by God of his all-determinative reality. The "oneness" with God in self-consciousness is not an ontologistic participation, but is rather a situation, or relationship, of "communion" (*Gemeinschaft*)[56] between unequal partners, the lesser of whom is being "given" or "posited" in light of the absolutely determinative originality of the other.

The importance of Schleiermacher's philosophical description of humanity's self-consciousness in feeling as a unified "knowing" and "being" is especially evident in regard to the "feeling" of absolute dependence. As the locus of a person's existential relation to God, this feeling is to be understood as somehow both a "knowing" and a "being" with God. To be "knowing" God maintains the absolute distinction of the two, while to know "being" with God indicates the direct connection of the two. The distinction between the two is not overcome, even in the immediacy of the self's consciousness of God's effecting the self, because the existing self's position of "having" its determination makes it uniquely self-existent as well as absolutely dependent.

Because the feeling of self's dependence on God is ultimately ascertained as a "higher" feeling than the self's dependence on the world, Schleiermacher

---

[55]Ibid., #32, int.

[56]Ibid., #62,2.

often seeks to explain this felt distinction in more than just the terms of God's presence within the feeling—and this he does by suggesting that the God-consciousness leans more heavily into the *being* of feeling than into the knowing. The implication of his philosophical discussions of the feeling of absolute dependence often is that in that locus of one's feeling, the person is more involved in the self's *being* with God, than in knowing of God. (In the world-consciousness, by contrast, the knowing is more influential than the being.) The knowing-being continuum of feeling is so tilted toward being in the feeling of God-consciousness, because in it the person is appropriating the essence of one's knowing-being self in particular regard to its necessity to be.

A person realizes here, as Spinoza maintains,[57] that the nature of one's self is that it is determined in the position of coming to be, and that "being," more than knowing, is therefore that characteristic which is most directly involved in the transpersonal grant of personal existence. Even though the whole "self" and its "existence" through self-consciousness entail the mutual coinherence of being and knowing, what occurs in the God-consciousness is more the being than the knowing: a person finds that the self is more given for "being" with God than "knowing" God. One finds the self most determinately as a *conatus*, or a drive "to be," and this one can only fulfill by "being" in relationship to one's source.

In our subsequent theological reflection upon this "pious" mode of consciousness of absolute dependence, we will designate as "God" the source, or *Woher*,[58] of our being-knowing selves, and therefore also as the whence of the immediate consciousness of having an absolute source. We will discern that we are posited or determined as thinking beings by a "creative divine activity, . . . a

---

[57]Schleiermacher, *Outlines of A Critique of Previous Ethical Inquiry*, *Sämmtliche Werke* III,1 (32-35). Schleiermacher's appreciation of Spinoza's view of the human self was long-lasting, although in his later works he acknowledged that the Spinozistic view entailed a heavily universalistic absorption of the processing individual being into the totality of being.

[58]Schleiermacher, *The Christian Faith*, #4,4.

person-forming divine influence,"[59] that is the logos of creation, disposing and preserving all individual beings for their reunification in the ultimate reality. Inasmuch as God is also the source of the person's knowing, as well as being, God comes to the person in the feeling of absolute dependence as the word, or knowing, of being. Humans are importuned to *be* with God because the person *knows* both humans and the world to be absolutely dependent upon the divine. The logos of all being presents itself to human beings as the word of unifying love.

The God-Consciousness as Able to Comprehend the World-Consciousness

The God-consciousness, as one of the two potential sources of immediate self-consciousness, can now be understood as qualitatively distinct from and superior to the other potential source, that is the world-consciousness. This qualitative distinction is asserted by Schleiermacher because the very definition of God-consciousness is framed in terms of absolute dependence upon a whence both of the conscious self *and* of the entire world of relativity. The self's consciousness of the world and of their reciprocating dependence is projected as viable only because it is the subsidiary project of a higher consciousness, which absolutely transcends and unifies it. The God-consciousness transcends the world-consciousness, but in a fashion of fulfillment, not of destruction:

> Not only is the feeling of absolute dependence in itself a co-existence of God in the self-consciousness, but the totality of [worldly] being from which, according to the position of the subject, all [sensible] determinations of the self-consciousness proceed, is comprehended under that feeling of dependence; and therefore all modifications of the higher self-consciousness may also be represented by our describing God as the basis of this togetherness of being in its various distributions.[60]

The totality of all worldly being is not only interrelated in world-consciousness, but is also comprehended (*befässt*), or dealt with under the aegis

---

[59]Ibid., #100,2.

[60]Ibid., #30,1.

of the absolutely determinative consciousness. The God-consciousness reveals God as the absolute origin and continuing basis (*das Begründende*) of finite being, not as a logically *a posteriori* synthesis or pantheistic *Aufhebung* of the elements of being. World-consciousness comes to be seen *sub specie aeternitatis*, but only because God-consciousness has in its own way informed the self as to the ultimate source of even the world and the consciousness induced by it.

The multiple relativities of worldly consciousness are seen by contrast with the unifying higher consciousness to reduce individual beings to antithetical objects.

> In the feeling of absolute dependence, the antithesis [of self and other] again disappears and the subject unites and identifies itself with everything which [in the world-consciousness] was set over against it.[61]

The feeling of absolute dependence enables us to accept that in the one, we and all other sensible things are unified and identified together as absolutely dependent, even in our variegated relativity. The relativities and distinctions of individual entities are thus transformed *in the light of* the higher consciousness, but the disparities within world-consciousness are not able to affect the unified simplicity of the consciousness of absolute dependence.

> The highest self-consciousness is no wise dependent upon outwardly given objects which may affect us at one moment and not at another. As a consciousness of absolute dependence it is quite simple, and remains self-identical while all other states are changing.[62]

The question of *how* the God-consciousness and the world-consciousness, with their totally distinct origins, are able to co-exist as reciprocally related potentials of consciousness will be delayed for consideration under the heading of "actual moments" of conjoint consciousness. Our effort to this point has been to

---

[61] Ibid., #5,1.

[62] Ibid., #5,2.

show that Schleiermacher conceives these two potencies of consciousness as ontological elements of the self-as-conscious, which must be hypothetically categorized in order to understand their structure of potentiation into one full existence of actual self-consciousness. Certainly his philosophical usage in setting up a working ontology of human consciousness has often been more confusing than illuminating, but we have attempted to clarify the issue by moving beyond the surface of existential ontology to the definitive metaphysical certitudes of self, world, and God—which Schleiermacher obviously believed to underlie all existential manifestations of self-conscious feeling.

The Philosophically Absolute Category of the "Transcendental Ground"

The key to Schleiermacher's understanding of the reality of self-consciousness is his conception of *each* potential component of consciousness as an ontologically real exemplification of the ideal-real polarity which characterizes all finite reality. The worldly self-consciousness is thus just as "real" as are the essential self and world whose reciprocal relationship it brings to consciousness. Further, the Godly self-consciousness is just as real as the essential self and its non-reciprocally related source in God. The question that then presents itself for our reflection is why should a God who is absolutely related to his creation of world and selves also dispose himself to be related to the selves in a further mode of self-conscious reality. The answer to this "why," says Schleiermacher, is certainly hidden in God's all-determinative creative will, but it is not hidden from us to discern the "how" by which God absolutely relates himself to us and to all creation.

Both philosophy and theology are led to understand, in their respective fashions, that there *is* an absolute determinative source of all creation, and that it is the unity underlying and transcending the given polarity of the real-ideal creation. Philosophy perceives through dialectical reasoning that there should logically be a unitary source of the dialectical polarity of nature and reason found in the created world. Theology, with its more subjective approach to the perception of reality, perceives in the reality of human self-conscious feeling a unitary source, that has made possible both the reality of the self's feeling-life and the reality of the world surrounding the self.

In the philosophical view of creation, both self and world are constituted as polar ideal-real entities, implying a transcendental source or ground to give them the essential unity in which the coinhering polarity transpires. In his most purely speculative philosophical work, the *Dialectic*, Schleiermacher provides a reasoned explanation of how the dialectical co-inherence of the real and ideal aspects within all entities must be derived from a transcendental disposition of the individual's essential unity, which disposition must be effected by a singularly unitary source. The ideal-real polarity is seen throughout the world as the interaction of reason and nature, while it is seen in the self as the interaction of knowing and being, or of thinking and willing.[63] In both world and self, the polar unity of the finite being points to a "transcendental ground, itself by virtue of which alone our being—as thinking that is willing, and willing that is thinking—can be one."[64] The kind of "principle," or transcendental ground, that could provide for duality within unity is finally ascertained at best by philosophy as the logical "presupposition" (*Voraussetzung*)[65] of dialectical thought and reality.

We can best understand this speculative ontology of polar reality by looking at ourselves, says Schleiermacher, because the pattern of all reality is most "immediately" present to us as we look through the self-consciousness at the underlying "real self" (*Eigenthümlichkeit*). The immediate self-consciousness, or feeling, is a person's way of "having himself,"[66] and the self one ascertains is of a type with all other reality, that is, a polar unity of reason and nature. But in the self-conscious status of "having" oneself, human beings are distinguished from all other real entities in that they ascertain the absolute unity of determination from

---

[63]Schleiermacher, *Dialektik*, (Odebrecht) 287.

[64]Schleiermacher, *Dialektik*, (Jonas) 430.

[65]Schleiermacher, *Dialektik*, (Odebrecht) 271.

[66]Ibid., 287.

which all realities, including humans, have come. In contrast to the reflective consciousness of philosophy, the immediate self-consciousness of feeling finds itself *more* than logically aware of the absolute source and ground: immediate self-consciousness finds that one aspect of its "self-having" is the self-consciousness of being utterly "posited" by the absolute.

> This transcendental determination of [immediate] self-consciousness constitutes the religious side of the same, or the religious feeling. In it the transcendental ground or the highest being is itself represented.[67]

How does it happen that the self's subjective "self-consciousness" can be just as totally determined by the transcendental ground as can the objective, metaphysical realities of self and world? Obviously, says Schleiermacher, only because the transcendental ground chooses to constitute and to determine the just-as-real dimension of "self-conscious" reality that is characteristic of human beings—making it as real in accordance *sui generis* of conscious existence, as are the self and the world real *sui generis* of metaphysical essence. Humankind is uniquely constructed within the range of reality as a distinct entity not only of selfhood, but also of immediate self-consciousness, in which the determinacy of both human realms of constitution is immediately presented to people. The self "has" itself *qua* constituted by an absolute source of determination, but also by the relative source of the finite world—which is in turn also under the original absolute determination.

The Absolute Qualitative Distinction between the Feeling-Self and the Transcendental One

By determining the *essential* self as a knowing being, God also determines the *self-conscious* potency for knowing being and being knowing which becomes the representation within self-consciousness of that original absolute determination

---

[67]Schleiermacher, *Dialektik,* (Jonas) 430.

of the self. The confusing suggestion in the subjectivist-idealist interpretation of Schleiermacher is the identity-type of conceptualization of the relationship between finite self-consciousness and the infinite ground of all reality. After his apparent early leanings toward identity theory, Schleiermacher definitely asserts in the *Dialectic* and in *The Christian Faith* that human self-conscious reality in feeling is not only *not* identical with the absolute, but that it is in complete antithesis to it. The most singular side of self-consciousness, in fact, is that in which the person "feels" the absolute *otherness* of the determinative source that coposits itself along with the human self in the consciousness. Whatever or wherever that determinative source may be, and however it effects its absolute commands, Schleiermacher seems to say, it is clear that it sets out (effects) the full ontological constitution of a person's selfhood and self-consciousness so that one can immediately ascertain the source as absolutely transcendent and as *totaliter aliter*.

The absolute determination of the person's essential being-knowing self is translated by people into the peculiar existential consciousness of absolute dependence. Yet between the metaphysical *source* of one's absolute determination and one's existential *sense* of absolute dependence, there lies an "infinite qualitative distinction," and here Schleiermacher foreshadows Kierkegaard, even as he rehearses Calvin, Luther, and Augustine. The absolute transcendence of God, which is somehow actually revealed to relative human beings, is the theological *prius* that Schleiermacher endeavors to affirm even in his seemingly anthropocentric terminology of the "feeling of absolute dependence." The feeling of absolute dependence is the being-knowing consciousness *that* the transcendent "one" is there, but it is neither an ontological participation with the one nor a knowing grasp of the one *a se*.

Schleiermacher indeed follows not only his Protestant forbears, but also Augustine again, in holding up the transcendent source and origin as the absolute determinant of all that is. God is seen by Schleiermacher more as absolute "will" than as absolute being or absolute knowledge. Reality (including the world and humankind) is definitively what it is because God is absolute will (or cause, or determination), thereby enabling reality as the polarity of knowing-being to live in its dependent relationship to the source of its absolute determination.[68] Finite reality enjoys the life and plentitude which it does, not because it is indwelt by God (Aristotle), nor emanated from God (Plotinus), nor extended from God (Spinoza). Reality becomes itself, rather, because God wills it so, and Schleiermacher takes great pains to distinguish his view from the immanentistic and pantheistic suggestions of other thinkers. Indeed, the Augustinian emphasis on the willful transcendence of the absolute source and origin is what places Schleiermacher as much in the dialectical Augustinian approach to theodicy as in the developmental Irenean approach, as John Hick[69] seems to overlook in his rendition of the Schleiermacherian theodicy.

Schleiermacher's fundamental belief that the transcendental source is known *qua* absolute only to immediate self-consciousness, and not to reflective consciousness, is asserted not only in his theology but in his philosophy as well. In the *Dialectic*, he presents the transcendental ground as the logical presupposition of the dialectical unity of nature and reason in all reality. At the same point, however, he asserts that this speculative metaphysical formula is in no way revealed to reason, as it is to feeling in the feeling of absolute dependence. Human beings may be given no more *access* to the absolute through pious feeling than through reason,[70] but they are given a *certainty* of its originative determinacy in the immediate existential reality of their feeling.

In his theological writings, therefore, Schleiermacher first points out that only theological reflection upon the redeemed self-consciousness is able clearly to distinguish itself from self-limited philosophical reflection, which is not open

---

[68]Schleiermacher, *The Christian Faith*, #55.

[69]John Hick, *Evil and the God of Love* (New York: Harper, 1966).

[70]Schleiermacher, *Dialektik*, (Jonas) 152.

to the ultimate truth contained in pious feeling.[71] In their sinful state, humans limit themselves to the feelings of the dominant world-consciousness, and to philosophical reflection upon only the relative dialectical unity of the world. Even when one passes out of the sinful state and opens oneself also to the feelings of God-consciousness, however, one still realizes, as is suggested in the *Speeches* and in the *Dialectic*, that philosophical reflection upon the relative unity of the world *per se* can never yield more than a relative, immanental principle of its source and origin. Only pious reflection upon the feeling of an absolute determinative source of both world and consciousness can yield a totally transcendental view of God, as absolutely "other" than all the dialectical interrelations of finite reality.

Schleiermacher seeks to contradict those who would derive only through philosophical deduction a pantheistic sort of dialectical unity from the world's relative polarities, and thereby slide over the deeper insight into absolute unity provided in feeling:

> The feeling of absolute dependence is not to be explained as an awareness of the world's existence, but only as an awareness of the existence of God, as the absolute individual unity.[72]

Feeling is opened beyond the world, as reason is not. Feeling does comprehend the world, in the self's consciousness of relative dependence and relative freedom toward the world, but feeling also comprehends beyond the world, to the absolute unity of its and the world's common determination.

> The world, if we assume it to be a unity, is nevertheless in itself a divided and disjointed unity, which is at the same time the totality of all contrasts and differences. . . . To be one with the world in self-consciousness is nothing else than being conscious that we are a living

---

[71]Schleiermacher, *The Christian Faith*, #32,3.

[72]Ibid.

part of this whole; and this cannot possibly be a consciousness of absolute dependence; the more so that all living parts stand in reciprocal interaction with each other.[73]

In pointing out that the feeling of absolute dependence is derived from a source of absolute unity, not from a synthetic unity such as the world, Schleiermacher effectively dismisses those who would regard his view as pantheistic or immanentistic. Especially in reply to Rudolph Otto, who regarded the feeling of absolute dependence as not qualitatively different from the feelings of relative worldly dependence,[74] Schleiermacher would likely have emphasized that the absolute-dependence feeling is a knowing-being instantiation of the absolutely singular determination of the self. The feeling of absolute dependence, therefore, can "solely refer to *one* highest reality," (*nur auf "ein" höchtes Wesen beziehen*)[75] as utterly transcendent in determining the utter "thatness" of the self. As the self's singularly unified (*ein*) determinant, it is held in absolute distinction from the multiple worldly relations of the self's constitution.

The fact that the absolute presents itself as the *determinant* (*Bestimmende*) of the self's finite consciousness of *determination* (*Bestimmtheit*) cannot mean that the absolute is not an infinitely distinct and self-existent reality; it rather means quite the opposite. Schleiermacher clearly considers this reality to be "the determinant outside of self-consciousness"[76] which is "the absolute divine causality (*Ursächlichkeit*) that corresponds to our feeling of absolute dependence."[77]

---

[73]Ibid.

[74]Rudolph Otto, *The Idea of the Holy*, J. Harvey, trans. (London: Oxford University Press, 1970) 9.

[75]Schleiermacher, *The Christian Faith*, #8,2. (Emphasis in the original.)

[76]Ibid., #30,1.

[77]Ibid., #79,1.

The Conjunction of God-Consciousness and World-Consciousness within the Actual Self-Consciousness as Not Implying an Identity of the Two Sources of Consciousness

If Schleiermacher indeed believes that God is absolutely transcendent in his aseity, and that human God-consciousness is absolutely distinct from the world-consciousness, why does he sometimes use terminology which seems to blend, if not to confuse, the two aspects of conscious dependence:

> Not only is the feeling of absolute dependence in and for itself a co-existence of God in the self-consciousness, but the totality of [worldly] being from which, according to the position of the subject, all determinations of the self-consciousness proceed, is comprehended under that feeling of dependence.[78]

The context in which this conjunction and co-mingling of the two levels of self-consciousness so often occurs is in the actual moments of self-conscious existence, in which the two potential sources are no longer *pre-suppositionally* considered as *separate* components of the actuality of consciousness. But when Schleiermacher refers to the world-consciousness, and to the God-consciousness, "in and for itself" (*an und für sich*) he obviously is presupposing that each potential has a separate source of determination, even though as actualized moments of feeling they come to occur together.

A generic ontological analysis of existence seems to be what Schleiermacher is proposing when he speaks of the two structural potentials of human existence as "universal" (*allgemein*),[79] "fundamental" (*wesentlich*),[80] and necessarily "presupposed" (*vorausgesetzt*),[81] as contained in every actual moment of

---

[78]Ibid., #30,1.

[79]Ibid., #33.

[80]Ibid., #33,2.

[81]Ibid., #32.

human existence (*Dasein*). Unlike the turn toward subjective idealism taken by Heidegger in his later ontology of *Dasein*, however, Schleiermacher insists that the ontological elements are co-posited (*mitgesetzt*)[82] into the existential setting by distinct outside determinants.

The God-consciousness and the world-consciousness are seen as universal ontological constituents of the pattern of all human *Dasein* because they are the two potencies manifested in every particular moment of actualized *Dasein*. They are actually experienced in the self's existence only as conjoined, but their separate derivations are also constantly presented, and therefore must be ontologically presupposed and categorized.

The God-consciousness as the existential potency derived from the absolute determination is clearly called a fact (*Tatsache*)[83] or element (*Element*)[84] of self-consciousness, which as "an inwardly permanent given" (*ein innerlich immer Gegebenes*), nevertheless "can be made apparent at any moment"[85] of actualized consciousness. As a constituent ontological element of a person's existence, it remains always (*immer*) what it is, regardless of the shifting dispositions made of it, as it is conjoined with world-consciousness in actual finite moments of existence.[86] Schleiermacher insists on the ontological potency of God-consciousness as a real fundament of existential life, and not simply as a nominalistically designated presupposition. God-consciousness *per se* must be considered as a separately known potential element exactly *because* it is also a conjointly known participant in self-consciousness:

---

[82]Ibid., #4,4.

[83]Ibid., #29,1.

[84]Ibid., #66,1 & #33.

[85]Ibid., #35,1.

[86]Ibid., #33,1.

> The immediate feeling of absolute dependence is [both] presupposed [ontologically] and actually contained [existentially] in every Christian religious self-consciousness.[87]

The God-consciousness must be ontologically identified and categorized according to its distinct absolute derivation, but it must also be existentially recognized as potentiating only within actual moments of conjoined world-consciousness.

> What emerges in actual consciousness, under whichever form of the antithesis [of worldly pleasure and pain], as God-consciousness, is always what has already been described, namely, the feeling of absolute dependence, and . . . no modification of the God-consciousness can be instanced where this feeling might either be absent or have added to it anything except what is related to and constitutes the [worldly] antithesis in question. The feeling of absolute dependence never purely by itself [potentially] fills a moment of religious experience. . . . As often as the indwelling [*einwohnend*] God-consciousness seeks to emerge, it appears either as advanced or arrested [by the world-consciousness] in its functioning.[88]

When Schleiermacher moves from structural (*existenzial*) ontology into his phenomenology of the actual (*existenziell*) moments of existence-feeling, he points out that "this God-consciousness does not constitute by itself alone an actual moment in religious experience, but always in connection with other particular [sensible] determinations."[89] It is more apt, therefore, when sorting out Schleiermacher's terminology, to take "an actual moment of pious feeling" as more specifically correct than the generalized ontological "pious feeling," or "God-conscious-

---

[87]Ibid., #32.

[88]Ibid., #62,2.

[89]Ibid., #32,1.

ness," or "feeling of absolute dependence." In this way, it is made clear that in a given moment the potential for God-consciousness may become actually dominant over the potential for world-consciousness, since either can be actually known only in such actual interface. When the opposite state of consciousness occurs, it is nonetheless clear that the dominant world-consciousness can never completely overcome the God-consciousness, or the "spirit" which is "implanted"[90] in the self-consciousness.

> Since the spirit's demand is always the same, the spirit itself, wherever it is less able to work [actually] effectively, appears as a baffled and defeated force [potential], and the subject therefore as in a state of sin.[91]

Regardless of its alternation in being actualized at the forefront of self-consciousness, the God-consciousness is seen as one of the two constant potentials without which self-conscious life would have no content, derivation, or reference. It is to the existential process of the composite actualizing of the potentials that we now turn.

ACTUAL SELF-CONSCIOUSNESS

Introduction to Actual Self-Consciousness

The immediate self-consciousness has for Schleiermacher the elemental ontological structure of the two potencies, "world-consciousness" and "God-consciousness," issuing conjointly into one integral actuality, or "actual self-consciousness." The two potencies in fact are understood as presuppositionally implicit in the more fully phenomenal and consciously manifest locus of actualization. Actual self-consciousness is the conjoint manifestation of the two

---

[90]Ibid., #94,2.

[91]Ibid., #67,2.

potencies for self-consciousness, which are themselves representative of the God-determination and the world-determination of the essential self. Actual self-consciousness is the specific reality of existence (*Dasein*), in which the self is posited as replicating the underlying God- and world-determined essential self (*Wesen, Sein,* or *Eigenthümlichkeit*). Actual self-consciousness is thus designated by Schleiermacher as the focal element in the complex structural ontology of immediate self-consciousness, or feeling. But at the same time, he indicates that in this abstractly-generalized ontological "locus" we actually find the specific, ontic instances of existential life-process.

The "actual self-consciousness" thus may be categorized in an ontologically general way, but only because it is first manifested in the empirical descriptions of the specific, concrete moments which are actual feelings. The complex ontological structure of reciprocally-dyadic potentials, feeding into the unifying actuality of self-consciousness, can be known only implicitly through the definitely explicit content of the actually processing moments of life. The ontological category of "actual self-consciousness"[92] is really a general extrapolation from the concourse of specific ontic moments of existence, "the connection of our actual living moments" (*den Zusammenhang der wirklichen Lebensmomente*).[93] Every actual moment is unique, but each is the presentational activity (*vorstellende Tätigkeit*)[94] of the same, continually ingressing potencies, and therefore all "moments" imply the ontological continuity of a central place (*Ort*),[95] which is the self-in-actual-self-consciousness.

---

[92]Ibid., #34,1.

[93]Ibid., #11,2.

[94]Ibid., #34,1.

[95]Ibid.

"The actual individual self-consciousness" (*das wirkliche einzelne Selbstbewusstsein*)[96] is the ontological locus wherein and whereby the fully true and fully real instances of existence actually transpire. The most real and most concrete unit of existence, of human life, is thus a *Moment*[97] of the actualizing self-consciousness, or what Schleiermacher also calls a specific excitation (*Erregung*),[98] stirring (*Bewegung*),[99] emotion (*Gemütserregung*),[100] or affection (*Affekt*).[101] Each of these terms is used by Schleiermacher to indicate the singular but integral unit of inner experience (*innern Erfahrung*)[102] which is an act (*Akt*)[103] of "actual self-consciousness."

When Schleiermacher speaks of actual self-consciousness as a "place" (*Ort*) that is "there" (*da*),[104] he seems to consider the self *qua* feeling, or existence, as more ontologically definite than the chimerical inward self of later existentialist thinkers. The reason for Schleiermacher's greater ontological definition would seem to be that for him the existing of actual self-consciousness is not a solipsistic flash of freedom, but is rather the substantive product of underlying ontological positings, which place it as a positer. Immediate self-consciousness is real because it is the actual conjunction of the two conscious potentials, which in their way represent the underlying determinants of the self. "The actual

---

[96]Ibid., #110,3.

[97]Ibid.

[98]Ibid., #55,3.

[99]Ibid., #74,2.

[100]Ibid., #32,1.

[101]Ibid., #3,4.

[102]Ibid., #30,2.

[103]Ibid., #66,2.

[104]Ibid., #11,2.

STRUCTURAL ELEMENTS OF IMMEDIATE SELF-CONSCIOUSNESS 73

individual self-consciousness" shows itself in every "moment"[105] as the bringing together of the two potentiating forces, which somehow combine into a complete experience of the "self's having itself," according to its underlying dual constitution. Thereby is given to the self "a coexistence [*Zugleichsein*] of the two in the same moment (and) this relatedness . . . in the unity of the moment is the consummating point of the self-consciousness."[106] This "consummating point" (*Vollendungspunkt*) is the "complete" or "full" presence to the actually self-having self of the determinative powers which make it what it is.

> The combining of potency and actuality, put in a fundamental sense, is the essence (of the self); the same combination in particularity is its existence.[107]

This rather explicit ontological formulation of the essence and the existence of the self is able to be expostulated only upon the basis of empirical examination of actual moments of self-consciousness, however, and could in no way be logically deduced by either speculative dialectic or speculative ethics, for which it would only be conjecture.[108] But existential actuality does in the facts (*Tatsachen*) of feeling present itself as just such an integrated conjunction of fundamental potentialities, and it is at the instance of the empirical evidence of these actual, ontic, moments that Schleiermacher is prompted to reflect with whatever ontological generalizations he develops.

---

[105]Ibid., #110,3.

[106]Ibid., #5,3.

[107]Braun & Bauer, II, *Ethik*, 533.

[108]Ibid., 540 (#73).

The Ontological Status of Actual Feeling

Schleiermacher's rather philosophically couched ontological propositions seem to be deliberately modest in extrapolating only from the empirically-given moments of actual self-consciousness. The basic impetus behind his entire program of philosophical ontology seems simply that of emphasizing self-conscious existence, or feeling, as being ontologically distinct, because it "has" not only its own being, but also the determinative influences of other reaches of reality.

> We always have the God-consciousness with the [sensible] consciousness of the togetherness of all [worldly] being in our [immediate] self-consciousness, and that in the moment in which our being is joined with being outside ourselves.[109]

The crucial question which later analysts have put to Schleiermacher naturally has been that of how and why the distinctively "other" realities of God and world may in any sense be said to be present to, or determinative of, the existential reality of human self-consciousness. But the metaphysical polarity of subject and object, and the epistemological polarity of religion and revelation, are quite often imposed upon Schleiermacher's polarity of self and other, as if to insinuate that such a polarity endemically involves radical contradiction, to the detriment of reciprocity. The assertion that *two* situations of reciprocity between self and an outside other can be realized reciprocally (conjointly) in the moments of actual self-consciousness seems to many to stretch the possibilities even of dialectic beyond comprehension.

Yet it is this dialectical conjunction of two already dialectically constituted patterns of self-other relationship which Schleiermacher does indeed claim to discern within immediate self-consciousness. And it is because of their radically different origins in God and in world that Schleiermacher is led to maintain that only the peculiar recapitulative actualizing of existence could reveal both the

---

[109]Schleiermacher, *Dialektik*, (Odebrecht) 301.

patterns as already determinative of the essential self. Thus the full actuality of immediate self-consciousness is translated by Schleiermacher as "feeling," "existence," or "experience"—not in the perjorative sense indicated by later interpreters, who view such terms as unilaterally subjective, but in the affirmative sense of "having the self,"[110] both in its selfhood and in its outside determinateness.

The particular moments of actual existence indeed are the explicit situation in which the self lives out its full knowing-being reality, which it has as constituted by the two types of determinants, God and world. The feeling-existence of "having oneself" occurs not as a solipsistic circle, but as a relational arc, in which the underlying self which we "have" is presented *qua* constitutionally determined by the outside sources of God and world. When these two contraposed determinants are together introduced as potentials also for determining self-consciousness, they are found as only subjectively *co-ordinated* by the existing self into concrete actual moments. Even in this context of subjective re-actualization in existence, therefore, neither loses its mark of origination in ontological reaches entirely beyond the self. And when the God-consciousness ultimately gains ascendancy in the moments of self-consciousness, this certainly would never suggest to Schleiermacher that the "religious experience" of the existential self could be self-constituted, without the actual "revelation" of the outside "one," which gives to the self its sense of total ontological determination.

The later dichotomy between religion and revelation would never have occurred to Schleiermacher, because for him the pose of self-consciousness is defined as the self having itself in relation to the sources of its determination. The religious sort of self-consciousness is defined as those moments in which the absolute determination of self is effectively actualized in its potency for revealing the fact of its absoluteness to the existing self. The occurrence of God-consciousness within the self-consciousness is thus an unconditional revelation which the self can

---

[110]Ibid., 287.

only receive and actualize—not necessarily in its fullness, and sometimes by obscuring it, but never by obliterating it. The self does *not*, as Feuerbach was to imply, create or project its feeling of absolute dependence. Rather, it simply deals in its given existential-actualizing way with the absolute determination which is given as one potential in its fundamental constitution.

The feeling of absolute dependence is not a correlative *pas de deux* with world-feeling, with the self trying to escape its worldly finitude in a futile Sartrian-type of absolute existential self-assertion. On the contrary, Schleiermacher's view of existence is that mankind's relative world-consciousness is always given in radical distinction from the absolutely determined consciousness, which the person neither asserts nor understands, but which one must deal with in an actualization of either acceptance or denial. Existence-as-feeling for Schleiermacher is quite the opposite of the later existentialist view of self-absolutizing; indeed, it is really not even similar to Tillich's view of the correlation in existence between self-assertion and divine dispensation.

Rather, it is a view of the existing self as fully determined in its essential structure and composition, and as freely self-expressive only in the sense of living out its given pattern of determinations. The self as existing out of and because of absolutely prior determinations is indeed just the opposite of the self as independent, and able to determine its own track into the limitless void of freedom. The actual freedom of existence in Schleiermacher's view has been better understood by the phenomenologists of existence, who follow him in recognizing the self as able only more or less to authenticate the outside determinations which constitute its pattern of givenness.

The phenomenological description of actual moments of existence, which is Schleiermacher's methodological entree, begins with the very center of human reality, because through it is manifested the ontological potentiating of the outside sources of the self's determination. Schleiermacher indeed sets up existence with the utmost ontological firmness, as the definite actualization of definite potencies, in contrast to Bultmann, who later endeavors to set up existence in terms of bare possibilities which must be self-realized. The existential (*existenziell*) moment of actuality is much more real to Schleiermacher than are its ontological (*existenzial*) potentials, in contrast to the Bultmannian emphasis on ontological possibilities as fundamental. The ontological potentials are for Schleiermacher manifest only as fulfilled in the concrete actualizations of existence, and existence need not therefore imply the ever-suspended possibilities of selfhood reaching out for some remote fulfillment.

In further contrast, in examining the existential ontology of Heidegger, it might be observed that Schleiermacher would not have agreed with his presuppositional emphasis on ontological structures *qua* mere possibilities. The kind of ontology of *Dasein* set forth by Heidegger in his main work was not attentive to the actualized instantiations of existence, which Schleiermacher saw as the only fully real units of selfhood. The Heideggerian type of ontology was pursued by Schleiermacher only as an heuristic device for understanding the implicit sources of the person's being, even though they could never be deduced in their metaphysical aseity. The emphasis on the phenomenological description of actual moments of the self's feeling as prior to any ontological speculation about its background is laid out in the maxim which Schleiermacher quoted from Anselm as the frontispiece to the original version of *The Christian Faith*:

> Nor do I seek to understand in order that I may believe, but I believe in order that I may understand. For he who does not believe does not experience, and he who does not experience does not understand.[111]

The true ontological structures of existence could never be understood merely by philosophical deduction, says Schleiermacher, for the *kinds* of possibilities constituting the structure of the self are so radically diverse in their origination and operation, that they could never be discerned except in their dialectical conjunction in actual existence.

---

[111]Schleiermacher, *Der Christliche Glaube*, frontispiece.

"To believe" and "to experience" as characteristic descriptions of the act of existing indicates that for Schleiermacher the phenomenal act of selfhood is more real than the ontological "possibilities" seen in existence by Heidegger and Bultmann, and also more real than the cognitively reflective intentionality seen in the existential act by Husserl. An "actual feeling" for Schleiermacher is neither the struggle to actualize a "mere" possibility of existence, nor is it the subjective pose of constructive knowing, which in both Kantian and Husserlian phenomenalism epitomizes the existing self. For Schleiermacher, the actual life of feeling does more than to "construct" or to "intend" an object. It is the self's holistic disposition of itself as both a being and a knowing in relation to the "outside" others that have already constituted the self as it is.

The "others" of God and world are given to the self *as its two essential determinants* and *in its two existential potentials*, but not as they are in themselves. The reality of their determination of the self, and their potentiation into the self's "having" itself *qua* determined, is what imbues the "feeling of self-having" as participant also in reality. The realness which Schleiermacher finds in the self's feeling is thus characterized as neither subjectively constructed nor as objectively projected. It is instead the realness of relationship, which every other entity in the knowing-being creation also has with its world and with its creator. Self-consciousness is thus the actualizing, in the unique reality of existence, of relationships with the essential realities underlying the self. The critical question usually put to Schleiermacher, of whether "feeling" or "immediate self-consciousness" is "real," can only be answered if one is prepared to suppose that there is reality even beyond the rational level of critical supposition. For those willing to join Schleiermacher in that supposition, he then endeavors to describe that feeling-reality, as a total-experience relationship between the self and the determinants which enter into its composition.

The existential self is declared by Schleiermacher to be real, not in the same way in which the essential self of underlying metaphysical identity is real, but as the continuous reactualization of that self in a distinct, but not separate, mode of reality. The ontological continuity between the essential self and the existing self is *not* found, however, between the essential self and *its* underlying metaphysical determinants that posit it from positions of complete otherness. The determinants of God and world are related to the self only as metaphysically distinct positors, who conjointly (but under the absolute origination of God) posit the self as an essentiality which finds full reality in existentiality.

The essence and existence of the self are thus much closer in ontological status than are the metaphysized essence of self and its radically "other" metaphysical determiners. Essence and existence are inherently close enough so that existence can partake of the potencies conveyed into its actualization from the essential level of self. Existence, or self-conscious feeling, is thus seen by Schleiermacher as the posited capstone of the self's reality, and not as an accidental epiphenomenon to be overcome or controverted to pure essence.

In contrast to the somewhat derogatory estimates of the reality inherent to "existence" given later by Kierkegaard, Heidegger, Bultmann, and even Tillich, Schleiermacher begins modern existential theory by defining existence as the positive outcome of an entirely posited and positing self. Existence for Schleiermacher is not just a "state" of self-induced delusion, which must be overcome by rising (or falling back) to an essential selfhood: rather, existence is the oft-times confused, but always fully real, actualization of the fully real and determined essential self. Existence is neither the kind of "lapse from God" which Schelling had said, nor a self-projected escape from the physical world, as later proponents of "pure consciousness" would say. It is instead the ontologically viable positing by God and his world of a self which must re-activate both of its positing sources.

With this sort of determinate reality ascribed to the posited and actualized self, it is no longer necessary for apologists of "truth as subjectivity" to rush in to bolster Schleiermacher's putative romantic emphemerality by injecting "subjective feeling" with some sort of cognitive content. This style of apology by many of Schleiermacher's self-styled protectors has too often ended up by making his intuitionism into an idealism, with the feeling-self often seen as having immediate cognitive entree into the metaphysical absolute, in some style of idealistic ontologism. It is this sort of intellectualizing of "feeling" that colors the recent work of George N. Boyd on Schleiermacher,[112] and which seems to Boyd necessary in providing meaningful reality to what is otherwise only the amorphously self-derived situation of feeling. In contrast to Boyd's interpretation, it seems in light of this study that a fuller appreciation of the ontological grounding and existential actualizing of feeling as treated in Schleiermacher's entire corpus would establish feeling as exemplifying the same degree of reality as the complex knowing-being reality of the self that it replicates.

Actual Existence as the Becoming of the Self's Reality

Feeling, or the actualizing immediate self-consciousness, is seen by Schleiermacher as so inherently real because it embodies the same being-type knowing (instead of the objective-type knowing of a detached subject) as the essential self. To be and to know together in the same determinate pose of reality means that the self inherently finds itself as so given, and that its being is constituted by its knowing, and its knowing by its being. The *essential* self is irrevocably given as this co-inherent reality of knowing-being, and therefore the *existing* self finds itself at the once-removed level or "rehaving" this knowing that is being and this being that is knowing. Since feeling, or actual self-consciousness, is also simply given to humans as the unsought necessity of replicating, or re-having, one's knowing-being self, and its two sources of God and world, the feeling self finds itself as an agency that must embody together its respective determinations by God and by world.

In the position of mediating agent, which must conjointly actualize two distinct sources of causation, the feeling self thus realizes the determined freedom of combination which is assigned to it. No matter how it eventuates the two

---

[112]George N. Boyd, "The Doctrine of Original Sin and the Fall in the Theology of Friedrich Schleiermacher," 44-63.

opposing potencies that present themselves to it, it nonetheless does always receive their potentiation in every actual moment, and finds itself materially constituted by the particular knowing-being type of reality that each contributes to the determination of the self. The actualizing, existing level of self thus finds that it is given *qua* distinct in this pose, and is inherently real only as continually re-having, or "feeling," its dually determined self. Certainly, therefore, Schleiermacher saw this relationally determined existing self as both a posited and a positing reality, far beyond the merely self-determined positing which later existentialists were to discern in the inner-most core of selfhood. The self's essential relationship to its determinants is represented or symbolized in its existential feelings toward them, its way of having them again in actual moments of self-consciousness.

The component of self-consciousness in which the self feels its *absolute* determination is, first, a receptive knowing, which only knows that the determinant is absolutely beyond self and world, and it is at the same time an active being, which only responds in accepting the absolute determination. The other component of self-consciousness, the determination of self by *world*, is also manifested as a being-knowing stance in the self, but now as only a relative being and knowing relationship of self to world.

In the world-feeling, the self is conscious of a reciprocity of determination between itself and the world, in which both its knowing and its being affect the world, unlike the purely receptive relationship which the self has with the absolute. Our knowing-being relation to God is that of the absolute, simple, or utter (*schlecthinnig*) "thatness" of our self's reality, and in this aspect of the self's determination, it can neither "know" about nor "be" with the determining other, except in the merest way of acknowledgement and acceptance. But the reality of the determination by an absolute other is the ultimate basis of the self's essential reality, *and* of the existential reality which must merely but utterly represent the absolute.

As having the being-knowing self in feeling, we both are and know that we are, both together, and this as we have two different sources of determinations of the being-knowing. This pose, moreover, is not for Schleiermacher strangely alienated from the essential level of self, nor does it entail a vain self-determination somehow to "reconcile" or to "solve" the being of our knowing or the knowing of our being. The position of existence, or having the self in feeling, is inherently good, according to Schleiermacher, because it is indubitably real, as we find ourselves given to ourselves by an incontrovertible nexus of outside determinations.

Actual self-consciousness is our re-positing of the posited dialectical unity of the self: feeling is real, therefore, not because it is an *a priori* faculty of absolute "knowledge," nor an ontologistic *Anknüpfungspunkt* from absolute "being," but it is real simply because it is a recapitulation of the self which is determined as real in *both* being and knowing. Feeling is therefore the finite reality of the self's having its infinitely and finitely determined self—it is an actual, historical instance of created reality coming into its own, but in a way somehow reiterative of what has been given to it. In this sense, Schleiermacher is able to maintain that the condition and definiteness of our knowing-being relation to *God* is mediated through the *world*-conscious relationship to the God-in-man, Jesus Christ.

The feeling that is existing, or actual self-consciousness, is regarded as finite—not as an entry point into absoluteness, in either a romantic or an idealistic sense—because it is, like all other finite realities, a determined meeting-point between the absolute and the relative. As such a meeting-point, its basic nature is that of a respondent, of bearing the determinations of its sources, and of reprojecting them. The existing self as continually ingressed upon by the potentiating determinants is thus always defined as a process of becoming, of continuous but conditioned reactualization of the underlying sources of its knowing-being.

Existence as becoming, or self-consciousness as actualization of potentials, is a basic conceptual frame which Schleiermacher found first elaborated in

Spinoza, and which he found more and more expressive of his own views. The process of movement between what the human being is given to be, and what the person may be given to become, seemed to Schleiermacher to define the status and parameters of human selfhood. Existence as the effort to become what one essentially already is, seems the fundamental ontological concept supporting Schleiermacher's phenomenological view of the actualizing self-consciousness. The quality, or mode, of existential reality is that of striving, of making an effort, to recapitulate the structure of the essential self, and this quality of forced indefiniteness is what gives humans the existential sense of freedom in self-actualization. Existence is known and lived (as knowing-being) as utterly "thrown" at humanity, but at the same time it is given with a frame of determining reference that accompanies (*begleitet*) and continues through (*durchgeht*)[113] every moment of its process. Existence occurs as a project that humans must undertake, but they find it to be circumscribed and carried along by the definitive determinants of God and world.

The whole life of feeling is therefore defined ontologically by Schleiermacher as a succession of actual self-conscious moments, in which the self is reformulating itself in conjoint relationship to the two elements which together formulate the essential self. The existing self is called upon constantly to represent to itself, and thereby to re-synthesize with one another, the two disparate elements of the unitary absolute and the multifarious world. The challenge to the self is to accept and to portray the conjunction of two qualitatively distinct realities, which nonetheless *have* been brought together under the auspices of the greater, and which now insist to the self that they be quantitatively reciprocal in existence, even though they be qualitatively apportioned in essence.

The project of appropriately combining the unitary one and the diverse many in their mutual constitution of the self is both an insistent demand placed upon the self, and a unique gift bestowed upon each human as its distinctive mode

---

[113]Schleiermacher, *Dialektik,* (Odebrecht) 288-89.

of existence. Through the boon of existence human beings are given the chance to re-express the metaphysical pattern of reality, and to portray in themselves a particular exemplification of how the absolute God initiates and unifies all the manifold entities of the relative world.

Actuality as the Conjunctive Formalization of Potentials

Actual self-consciousness can now be seen as that ontological domain of selfhood in which the two basic potentials of God-consciousness and world-consciousness are brought together in the form of existent actual consciousness. The two constitutive elements are seen as potencies (*Potenzen*), much in the equivocal Aristotelian sense of being at once strictly *potential* and fully *powerful* to effect their own potentiation. The potencies for actual-consciousness are seen by Schleiermacher as the material or substantive principles of the self-consciousness, which thereby provide the potentiating "whats" for the formalizing "how" of the actualization.

Since the God- and world-determinations of the essential self entirely provide these substantive potentials for the existing self's consciousness, it is in keeping with the Aristotelian outlook that the existing self can provide only the formal composition, or the actualization of the given potentials.[114] *That* the existing self is real, *why* it is real, and *what* it really is—all these principles of

---

[114] The other two of Aristotle's four causes, the efficient and the telic, are implied by Schleiermacher to reside also in the absolute, or divine, determinant of the self. The reality of the self's feeling-existence is thus attributed to God in three out of four of its causes: the efficient, the telic, and the material (inasmuch as God is ultimately the source even of the worldly potential itself). In the reality of feeling, therefore, this leaves only the formal cause as being contributed by the self, and not directly by God. At the level of the *essential* self's reality, of course, Schleiermacher would say that God is completely determinative of the self in every respect, including its essential form.

The Aristotelian backdrop to Schleiermacher's psychology of actualizing potentials is best presented in the *Psychologie*, 33-38. The description of God-consciousness and world-consciousness as potencies (*Potenzen*), and of existing actual self-consciousness as actuality (*Wirklichkeit, Tätigkeit*) is found in various of the philosophical works already cited, as well as in *The Christian Faith*.

existence are provided by the God-determination, (and part of the substantive whatness by the God-given world-determination). Only the *how*, or the formal actualizing of the other given principles, is constituted autonomously by the self in its stance of existence. Actuality-as-existence is real for Schleiermacher because it is the actualization of determinant potentials of selfhood, which are originated efficiently and teleologically beyond the self—in such an ontological pattern that the self is "made" for actualizing them.

God, and the world of God, are the direct *determinants* of the reality of every self, but only of the *essential* or metaphysical self. Only as *determinations* of the potentials of self-consciousness do they help constitute actual *existence*, thus disallowing themselves as immanent, immediate, or ontologistic constituents of actual self-consciousness. The life of *existing* selfhood is efficiently and telically caused by God, but only indirectly, in God's determination of the underlying essential self, which then potentiates into the actualized form of feeling-consciousness. Because God also essentially causes the world and its contributing determination of the essential self, it is God's direct effective and telic will that his and the world's conjunctive determination of humankind become potentiated by humans in the unique way of re-having themselves that is actualizing self-consciousness. With such a complete scope of determination attributed to God, the question inevitably put to Schleiermacher is that of *how* the determined self manages to be distinctly real, just at the level of formal, self-having actualization.

The meaning and reality of human freedom is certainly a critical question in any interpretation of selfhood, and it becomes apparent in Schleiermacher's ontological format that freedom must be understood in the rather conditional process-terms of formal actualizing of substantially determinate potentials. The potencies are given efficiently and telically as the substantive constituents for self-consciousness, because they represent into conscious existence the substantive determinations of the essential self by God and by world. Existence thus is manifested as the determinately climactic process of the potencies becoming actualized—of the self recapitulating its underlying *determinations*, but not the entirely "other" determinants of self.

This conditional, or relational, meaning of existential actualization by the self is in keeping with Aristotle's modest view of the freedom that the actualizing entity can exercise over its potential, although in Schleiermacher's bi-polar view of determination there are *two* potencies which present themselves to be conjointly actualized. The self-having actualization that defines existence is therefore seen by Schleiermacher to ontologize freedom to the extent that it *is* a *self* which exists *a se* as formally actualizing potentials for existence. It is not, therefore, the determinants of the potentials, as God or as world, that directly exist in the self. The self in self-consciousness does feel, or exist, or stand out of its potencies in a relatively free way, but only in the formal mode of *how* to actualize its potencies, not that, why, or what they are so to potentiate.

The assertion that the self is finitely and distinctly conditioned in its stance of existence is strongly affirmed by Schleiermacher's insistence that potentials are not themselves "realities," such as an immanentized presence of God or world *per se*, nor are they some kind of Platonically real essences to be immediately apprehended by the self. Rather, the potentials are but projections or extensions that convey the reality of the two determinations of the essential self into the existential reality of the actualizing self. The potentials are not merely nominalistically retrospected images of what may only be discerned from the actualized concretion of existence, but neither are they Platonically realistic as embodiments of the determinations of the essential self. Somehow, the "potentials" are understood as lying in process between the two categories of name and reality, and are designated simply as the conveyors of the real determinations of the self *qua* further constituent for self-consciousness.

The portrayal of self-consciousness as a reality of process, rather than a reality of substance, elaborates Schleiermacher's view of the potentials in their actualization as obtaining at the distinct ontological level of the *becoming* of self, in a way provided by the more *substantive* reality of the essential self. That such becoming occurs, as well as why, and with what components, is all posited to the self as the determination that it must somehow actualize its essential configuration in its own self-positing way. The existing self thus has itself *qua* utterly and relatively dependent on its two outside constituents, and could only imagine in a radically inverted way that it generates itself *de novo* or *ex nihilo*, in a purely formal process without constituent determinations. To feel or to exist, therefore, is to actually "have" in a reaffirmative way for oneself, the fundamental determinations of self that make it the reality that it essentially is.

The Coeval, Co-existent Conjunction of the Two Potencies in Actuality

In the style or manner in which the two potencies are presented into the moments of their actualization, Schleiermacher recognizes an ontological (structural) equivalence between them. Even though God- and world-consciousness are found to differ radically in their *material* derivation, they are given to the actualizing self-consciousness as *formally* coequal elements in the ontological composition of every existing moment. From within every experientially-given moment of self-consciousness, the two imploding potentials can only be "had" as formally similar, inasmuch as each provides separate material elements of the underlying dual determination of the essential self. Schleiermacher's most ontologically general description of an actual moment of self-consciousness is that it forms itself by the conjunction of the two different but equally implicit potential elements. The formal, ontological coequality of the two *existing* elements, that are given in material contrast at the level of their *essential* reality, is manifested in the dialectical reciprocity they attain at the level of actualization:

> It is impossible to claim a constancy for the highest self-consciousness [of absolute dependence], except on the supposition that the sensible self-consciousness is always conjoined with it. Of course, this conjunction [*Zugleichgesetzsein*] cannot be regarded as a fusion [*Verschmelzen*] of the two.... It means rather a co-existence [*Zugleichsein*] of the two in the same moment, which, of course, unless the ego is to

split up, involves a reciprocal relation [*ein Bezogensein beider aufeinander*] of the two.[115]

This polar reciprocity is exemplified, however, only in the formal context of the *existential* ontology, and does not for Schleiermacher reflect the substantive origins of the potentials in qualitatively opposite metaphysical sources of the self's essential determination. The implied question of how the absolute (divine) determinant and the relative (worldly) determinant can work together metaphysically, despite their radical qualitative distinction, to constitute the essential self, can only be speculatively answered by Schleiermacher in terms of the absolute's determining of and relating itself to all relativity. This sense of their ultimately absolute *distinction* becomes the substantive content of the existing self's actual feelings, but the actualizing self *qua* formalizing mediator receives and "conjoins" them both *qua* formally *similar* potencies for the moments of self-actualization. As potentials for feelings, as ontological elements of existing self-consciousness, they must be regarded as reciprocal *relata*, although as outpourings of their respective metaphysical powers, they carry the substance of radically contrasting sources.

> It is impossible for anyone to be in some moments exclusively conscious of his relations within the [worldly] realm of the antithesis, and in other moments of his absolute dependence in itself and in a general way; for it is as a person determined for this moment in a particular manner within the realm of antithesis that he is conscious of his absolute dependence. This relatedness of the sensibly determined to the higher self-consciousness in the unity of the moment is the consummating point of the self-consciousness.[116]

---

[115]Schleiermacher, *The Christian Faith*, #5,3.

[116]Ibid.

The distinction between the metaphysically absolute God and the ontologically relative human element of God-consciousness, which is only one potential element of the existential ontology of humanity, is suggested in many such passages as the following:

> If in any particular moment, God has determined part of self-consciousness, but this God-consciousness has not been able to permeate the other active [sensible] elements therein, thus determining the moment, the higher self-consciousness [is affected] with pain.[117]

That God-consciousness and world-consciousness are actually experienced as equal potentials for actual moments of self-consciousness is emphasized by Schleiermacher's repeated assertion of the inability of one to appear without the other. The "constant" occurrence of their "conjunction" could not be deductively discovered, but is simply that always self-evident empirical phenomenon which is the basic unit of self-conscious existence. It is precisely the permanent formal constitution by which the actual self is posited that makes it empirically certain of the seemingly paradoxical duality of its origination. Every actual moment of self-consciousness can but have itself as the formal conjunction of potencies, from two totally contrasting determinative sources.

> The feeling of absolute dependence, even in the realm of redemption, only puts in an appearance, i.e., becomes an actual temporal [*wirkliche zeiterfüllendes*] self-consciousness, in so far as it becomes aroused through and unites itself with another [sensible] determination of the self-consciousness. . . .[118]

---

[117] Ibid., #66,1.

[118] Ibid., #30,1.

The God-consciousness and the world-consciousness are always formally present in every "actual moment" (*wirkliche Moment*),[119] or every "actual self-consciousness" (*wirkliche Selbstbewusstsein*),[120] and in their continuing conjunction the two ontologically potential elements are formally constituted as the single ontological element of actuality, or the "entire course of our actual life-moments."[121] The "actual, individual self-consciousness"[122] manifests itself as the full-fledged ontological reality of human existence because each of its processing moments is composed of the formal conjoining of the two potential realities from the underlying essential self.

The fact that *two* qualitatively different potential elements seem both to be necessary for a full actualization of human consciousness, rather than a single potential moving toward actuality in the Aristotelian sense, can only be explained by Schleiermacher in the phenomenological observation that each would seem incomplete without the other. This observation applies, however, only at the phenomenal level of human existence, because it indicates that it is somehow the person's unique ontological position to need and to have the reciprocal polar tension between two absolutely distinct metaphysical principles.

At the metaphysical level of God and world *per se*, as they determine one's metaphysical selfhood, it is Schleiermacher's basic speculative deduction that there must be complete harmony, and no tension, between the completely different infinity of God and finitude of the world. Only at the existential level of human activity of "rehaving" these metaphysical *a priori's* does the person hold the multiplicious relativities of the world as somehow in dynamic tension with the unitary absoluteness of God.

---

[119]Ibid., #32,1.

[120]Ibid., #34,1, and #62,2.

[121]Ibid., #11,2.

[122]Ibid., #110,3.

The Actual Domination of Every Moment by One or the Other Potency

If the two potencies which are conjoined in actual consciousness are derived from the qualitatively different and proportionately aligned metaphysical powers supporting them, Schleiermacher must explain the process by which the potencies become formally equivalent in the polar tension of self-consciousness. The transition from the material essential level, of contrast-proportion between the determinative powers, to the formal existential level, of similarity-tension between them, is simply accepted by Schleiermacher as a further determination by the absolute power that the self should exist, as well as to subsist in its essence. Existence must be understood as the posited outcome of essence, and the existing self can have nothing but a sense of the determinate givenness of its effort to recapitulate its essence.

But the type of transition between essence and existence does somehow also mean that the formalized pose of existential "having" the potentiating powers of essential self becomes a non-essential rearranging of their original alignment. Within the formulation which is actual self-consciousness, the self finds not just the explicit powers of its outside determinations, but the implicit power of freely arranging them into configurations of reciprocal alternation and non-proportional representation.

It seems clear, therefore, that there is a definite ontological difference between the essential and the existential levels of the self, although certainly not a radical split. The dynamic of this transition is never clearly explained by Schleiermacher, and he seems here again forced to assume it simply as the positedness of the self in its total ontological dependence upon the absolute determinant. Schleiermacher's main conviction in this regard, therefore, continues to be that the pervasiveness of the absolute determination could not allow any real ontological breakage in the dependent world, not even in the special human status of existing self-consciousness.

Humans simply *find* themselves as given into the life of existence, in which they must formalize some sort of conjunctive relationship between two formally similar potentials. That the conjunction can neither be a fusion nor a perfect balancing seems also posited to humankind as a condition of the distinction between the two: the person can never in one's finite actuality comprehend or embody their infinitely proportioned distinction, but one must continuously *strive* to align them, according to the ambiguous comprehension in which the necessity for actualization places one.

Humanity's *existential* self-actualization thus positions the person between the God-potential and the world-potential, and in this conditioned and limited status the person is unable freely to know or to be oneself as one is in one's *essential* proportionate reference to both the absoluteness and the relativity. The person's enforced freedom of formalizing the potentials into conjoint momentary actualizations thus results in a shifting alternation of domination by one over the other, as the person strives to represent the perfectly proportionate domination of God-determination that obtains at the level of essential reality. Under this condition of essaying existence, the two originatively proportionate potentials become actually represented as struggling powers (*Grössen*)[123] or agents (*Agentien*),[124] which may attain to dominance of one over the other in any given moment of their conjunction.

The actualization is the formal bringing together of the two potencies, but their "coequality" must be seen simply as their common presentational urge for satisfaction, even though their reformulation may misrepresent their essential proportionality of absolute to relativity. The formal acts of existence thus bring together in a less than perfect alignment the two potencies of the metaphysically-distinct and proportionately-established principles of God and world. The type of *Potenz* here indicated is that of a subjectively-appropriated potentiality for

---

[123]Ibid., #67,2.

[124]Ibid., #66,2.

existing in consciousness, but also of one having the objectively-given power of its underlying determination to convey its substance into the momentous focus of ever-actualizing self-consciousness. The fact that no two actualized moments ever contain impulses of God and of world in quite the same combination accounts for the novelty, the ambiguity, and the determinative mystery of human life.

This off-centered alternation of dominance, which maintains existence always in a pose of uncertain tension, if not of struggle, seems to Schleiermacher as the only valid characterization to be made of how the two potencies reciprocally interact with each other. Although some interpreters have taken passages in Schleiermacher's basically philosophical works to mean that the forces and principles of life are in perfect dialectical balance, it is also evident in some of these works, even outside his specific phenomenological analysis of sin, that Schleiermacher recognized that the general structure of self-consciousness included the possibility of tension.

> There is nothing more to which the self is subject, except that in every moment a definite power is given to it as dominant . . . which is the result of the conflict between these different powers.[125]

In his work on psychology, he speaks of a pattern of predominance (*Vorzug*) among the factors of the self, which is indefinite in scope, and always subject to alternation (*Wechsel*).[126] Although in outright discussions of the significance of freedom, Schleiermacher may recognize that the particular domination (*Vorrang*) of a moment is due to the voluntary action (*Selbsttätigkeit*) of the individual,[127] freedom is usually understood as merely the formal actualizing of the given determinative powers. Humans find themselves in the juncture of every

---

[125]Schleiermacher, *Psychologie*, 11.

[126]Ibid.

[127]Schleiermacher, *The Christian Faith*, #69,2.

moment forced to accommodate two qualitatively different powers in the quantitative form of finite self-activity, so that the very form of existence is presented in a way which seems inherently impossible of perfect fulfillment.

The Dislocation of Actual Moments Leading to the Actuality of Sin

The admission of a problematic in existence seems to many interpreters of Schleiermacher to be inconsonant with the regularized structure that he assumes in his ontological analysis of the elemental constituents of such existence. That the determined elements of self-conscious *potentiation* could be so rendered by self-conscious *actualization* into a form unlike their essential arrangement, seems to many a feat of logical legerdemain in which necessity and freedom are impossibly transmuted. But Schleiermacher does indeed seem to be aware of the crucial difficulty here in his thought, and he tries in various ways to insist that the problem of transition from essence to existence is not just a logical anomaly, but is simply a phenomenologically discerned understanding of the given context of human reality.

Schleiermacher is certain only that the self is endemically caught in a reciprocal succession of efforts to express perfectly in existence the perfect structure of the essential self's determination. He maintains that the self can only acknowledge *that* it imperfectly strives to replicate that metaphysical order that is insistently presented by the impulsing potential elements; as to *why* existence is so imbalanced, the self can never finally distinguish between its own freedom of approach and the necessity of an impossible task imposed upon it. Humans can but give a phenomenological reading of their existential quest, and point through it to the absolute source of necessity that is revealed even within the ambiguities of that existence.

In the last analysis, therefore, it seems for Schleiermacher that the absoluteness of God must be maintained even to the extent of holding that every dimension of reality must be under his determination, even the misconstrued efforts of human existence to identify itself with the more essential dimensions of its reality. The actual misconstructions and disproportions that bring world-consciousness to be dominant over God-consciousness are indeed existentially real enough to be designated as "sin" and "evil," but they could never be essentially real enough to abrogate the real control of God over the ultimate fate of both mankind and world.

The reality of *sin*, as real instances of human self-actualization apropos its sources of determination, is understood by Schleiermacher as being of the same degree of reality as the *pious* instances of actualization. In both possible cases, the potencies are formally able to reach only a relative degree of predominance over one another. The position of existence in which this continual struggle for potentiation is manifested is thus understood by Schleiermacher as fully real, even in its fashion as an unconsummated effort to portray the underlying essence of the self's reality. Existence therefore is both real and good for Schleiermacher, because it is a direct, continuous outcome of the essential pattern of the self's created determination. Even as a confused, non-essential rendition of that ultimate order of determination, existence could never be seen as an estrangement from, or abrogation of, the absolutely determined self.

Such a dualism between existence and essence, as suggested by Kierkegaard and Barth, could never be accepted by Schleiermacher, in his view of the absolute divine control over every aspect of creation. Indeed, the very "non-being" of a radically dualistic evil, such as Barth proposes,[128] would seem to Schleiermacher an impossible interpretation of sin, which is real indeed because it *is* so closely related to the determination of God. Existence *per se* is good for Schleiermacher, because it is God's good gift of the recapitulation of our essential selves. It is not an accursed situation of non-being, even when it temporarily gives over to the misaligned actualizing of world-consciousness over God-consciousness.

---

[128]Karl Barth, *Church Dogmatics*, G.W. Bromiley and T.F. Torrance, trans. (Edinburgh: T. & T. Clark, 1958), vol. III/3, 351-52.

The structure of existence is actually given to us as our special position in reality, and it is the human process of self-disposition toward our essential determinations that makes human life for good or for ill. In the exis-tential situation of "servile freedom," in Paul Ricoeur's phrase,[129] the human being finds oneself responsible for carrying out a process of actualization which one also finds as implicitly fated to misconstruction. But because one of the determinations of self which potentiates into existence gives us to know that its absolute power is behind both our essential and our existential reality, we can but accept that our fate is the freedom of self-disposition in existence. It becomes apparent to the person, therefore, that he or she will never be able to conjoin in existence the powers of God-consciousness and world-consciousness in the perfect alignment of absoluteness and relativity that is found at the essential level of the self's determination. The two will always be somewhat out of joint, somehow in tension, because the human person's existential pose of self-actualizing is never sure of the essential scope of reality beyond its finitude.

> The feeling of absolute dependence never purely by itself fills a moment of religious experience, [but] as often as the indwelling God-consciousness really seeks to emerge, it appears either as advanced or arrested in its functioning.[130]

When the God-consciousness is advanced, we have a pious moment, but when it is arrested, we have a sensuous moment—the alternation of the determinative powers never completely settling into a constancy on either side. It is only within the context of existential recapitulation, however, that the world-consciousness and God-consciousness must strive against one another, and imperfectly attempt to replicate their natural alignment of the essential realm. But because the struggle involves the ascendancy of world-consciousness as well as

---

[129]Ricoeur, *The Symbolism of Evil*, 347.

[130]Ibid., #62,2.

of God-consciousness, Schleiermacher must view the struggle as that between two powers whose misalignment is a distinct contradiction to the essentially-determined proportion of God-domination over world.

> What gives a moment the character of sin is the self-centered activity of the flesh . . . for flesh is good when subservient to spirit, evil when severed from it.[131]

The question of *why* actual existence maldisposes the ontological potentialities given to it is for Schleiermacher a mystery ultimately lost in the absolute determination of the ontological status of actualization. One can only move on to a more empirical description of *how* the process of actualization historically carries out its alternation between ascendant states and stages of the respective potentials.

---

[131]Ibid., #74,1.

CHAPTER 3

THE STAGES OF DEVELOPMENT IN ACTUAL SELF-CONSCIOUSNESS

INTRODUCTION

States and Stages of the Actual Self-Consciousness

It is possible now to understand Schleiermacher's delineation of the ongoing life of immediate self-consciousness, for this is his tracing of the actual development of the conscious life as its fundamental components interact within their structure in varying patterns of struggle and fulfillment. Indeed, the ontological structuring of consciousness, already considered, usually remains for him an implicit, presuppositional (*vorausgesetz*) sort of backdrop for his explicit phenomenological examination of the unfolding process of actual consciousness at work. Yet, it has been our contention here that the "activity" of existence cannot be understood apart from the "structure" of existence, for "actual self-consciousness" so epitomizes both that its categoreal centrality in both makes it the linchpin of Schleiermacher's whole understanding of life.

The "actual self-consciousness," previously considered as the structural focus of the elements of immediate self-consciousness, is now to be considered as the dynamic focal point for combinations and recombinations of the potentiating elements of God-consciousness and world-consciousness, during the full course of life of the immediate self-consciousness. For Schleiermacher, moreover, it is *in situ* of an actual moment of the immediate self-consciousness that one always finds oneself at the initiation of any philosophical or theological reflection.

It is consequently his contention that every reflection that theorizes about the presuppositional structure of consciousness must have begun in the empirical presence of an actual moment of consciousness, whether it be one of sin or one of grace.

Actual self-consciousness for Schleiermacher is both an unchanging ontological element in the structure of existence and the ever-changing process of historical existence. In his empirical treatment of the formalizing process of actual self-consciousness, he therefore comes to focus upon the progression of "actual moments," as their temporal succession accumulates into what he calls "states" of existence, and finally into the "stages" of existence. The importance of so focusing with Schleiermacher upon the actualization *process*, for the study of sin and self-consciousness, will now be manifested, as sin is seen to be a fully realized state in the processing life of actual self-consciousness.

The most significant point to be made in this study of sin as a mode of "self-consciousness" is that sin is for Schleiermacher a most definite human reality just because it is such a state of the actualizing self-consciousness. Sin is just as signal a reality as is any other state of human life, because it is one basic form (*Lebensform*)[1] in which are conjointly actualized the potential elements of God- and world-consciousness. The two other basic "forms of life" for Schleiermacher are that which *precedes* sin, in humanity's original state of codetermination by God- and world-consciousness, and that which *follows* sin, in the state of redemption. Only by viewing all three as fully realized states of human life, moreover, can we understand Schleiermacher's view of the existential process that is "actual self-consciousness."

The "time" (*Zeit*)[2] of human existence is for Schleiermacher both quantitative and qualitative, that is, it involves both the actual putting together of the material components of self-consciousness and the formal manner of every combi-

---

[1] Schleiermacher, *The Christian Faith*, #107,1.

[2] Ibid., #67, int.

nation. Every "time" in one's life is both instantaneous and cumulative, for it involves each discretely realized moment, even as the succession of moments tends to accumulate into a certain type, or form. We can never escape either dimension, however, for we "have" our selves only as existing in particular moments, which yet do have greater tendencies to be associated in patterns of continuity.

Although Schleiermacher never fully elaborates a schema of the *existenzial* ontological elements that eventuate into actual *existenziell* moments, it seems clear that there is for him such an implied context that ties together both his philosophical and his theological reflections. It is quite possible to argue that he would have appreciated, if not supported, the later Heideggerian way of analyzing the structure and the process of existence. Although the contents and referents of Schleiermacher's *Existenzialen* (structural components) are quite different from those projected by Heidegger, Schleiermacher nonetheless seems to have set the pace for later existentialist thinkers when he talked about human existence as having both poten-tial structure and actual process. It has been our task so far to draw out a model of the *existenzial* structure that he presupposed, and it is now our task to picture this model passing through the *existenziell* process, which he presents only in fragmentary descriptions.

The quality of existing temporality, of actualizing one's potentials, is held up as that quality of the immediate self-consciousness that epitomizes human life. Every *Zeit* is both an actual moment (*Moment*) and the germ of a continuing state (*Zustand*). The steady succession of moments inevitable accumulates into various sorts of homogeneous states of existential time (*contra* Hume), in what Schleiermacher calls "the course of our actual life-moments" (*den zusammenhang der wirklichen Lebensmomente*).[3] This emphasis upon the continuity that develops even out of specific actualizations of consciousness is further indicated when he says that a continuous state is the aggregate of its actual quantitative increments,

---

[3]Ibid., #11,2.

"in whatever *measure* (the state) actually takes place during the course of a personality through time" (*in welchem Mass nun während des zeitlichen Verlaufs einer Persönlichkeit dieses wirklich vorkommt*).[4]

Even though the actual "moments" of self-consciousness are the ultimate units of existence, we find that they tend to group themselves into "states," which then enhance the continued preponderance of similar moments in an indefinite way. The fact that moments tend to so succeed themselves in streams of continuity is not, however, an ontological necessity implied in the potential structures of self-consciousness. Rather, it is only inferred *in loco* of an actualized moment that looks before and after itself at a likely pattern, or state, of continuation. It is from such a specific *existentiell* perspective that one usually comes to see many moments as having occurred as some sort of continuing "form of life," (*Lebensform*).[5]

That Schleiermacher sees an inevitable tendency toward the moments "repeating in time to proficiency,"[6] is evidenced especially in his usage of the term *Zustand* to refer to such habitually developed states of the actualizing self. *Zustand* is used by Schleiermacher in this sense more than its two synonyms of *Lebensform* and *Stand*,[7] but seems to draw even greater definition by analogy with them as the sort of existentially conditioned situation that could accumulate only in the course of actual self-consciousness.

A *Zustand*, or state, or condition, of the self-consciousness is thus a generic name for a somewhat continuous arrangement that may occur within the process of actualizing potentials. Schleiermacher speaks of "the inward *Zustand* as a

---

[4]Ibid., #4,4 (emphasis mine).

[5]Ibid., #107,1 and #108,6.

[6]Ibid., #67,2.

[7]Ibid., #74,1 and #111,3.

THE STAGES OF DEVELOPMENT IN ACTUAL SELF-CONSCIOUSNESS

whole,"[8] by which the actualizing self is seen characterologically in reference to moments both in its past and its future. Sometimes a condition seems to us "natural,"[9] but we may at any moment also "leave a condition behind."[10] Every *Zustand* involves a certain pattern of conjunction by the two potentials, but it will nonetheless always be open to further "principles of progressive development."[11] And even though every person has a unique inward dynamic in their own successive instantiation of various states, there are still enough similarities among our elemental human potentials to recognize that there will also be actual states that we all may hold in common.[12]

Because the "states" of consciousness do proceed along a "course," or line of development, during our lives, Schleiermacher recognizes such qualitatively temporal situations as having strongly conditioning effects upon all the situations that will succeed them. Not only do the states incur cumulative effects from the moments within themselves, but the states also provide an inevitably long-range cumulative effect upon those others that build upon them. No state, in other words, can ever be autonomously regarded as separate from its before or its after, but is ascertained as always holding within itself the influences of its past and the intimations of its future.

When the "states" of actual life are so regarded in a cumulative, coursing manner of succession, they will then also be understood as "stages," or levels, in a long-range process that can be understood only from the point at which the actual self-consciousness may be regarding itself. That "states" of the momentary consciousness should also be understood as "stages" is a judgment that Schleier-

---

[8]Ibid., #74,4.

[9]Ibid., #108,6.

[10]Ibid., #107,1.

[11]Ibid., #66,2.

[12]Ibid., #64,2, #11,2, and #91,2.

macher develops from his understanding of the existentiality of *Zeit*, which is both momentous and continuous. Thus a single moment, or *Zeit*, is always located in a context of moments, or a state, and as such defines the stage of life, or *Zeit* of life,[13] in which the person exists. The "time of life" in which a person may be is thus a staged sort of period, or a state that is actually cognizant of other states before and after,[14] even as it fully establishes its own character.

The most general term that Schleiermacher uses to refer to a period or stage in life is not *Zeit*, however, but is *Stufe*,[15] and he thereby seems to suggest an overall progression, or development, from lower to higher states of self-actualization. Thus he mentions different *Stufen*, in which the state of relative conjunction between God-consciousness and world-consciousness will vary in accordance with whichever is dominant.[16] From the perspective of the pious state, which regards itself as the ultimate stage in the life's actual course of development, all former states of more or less sinful dominance will be seen as but imperfect *Stufen*,[17] which were cumulatively developing toward readiness for the stage of redemption.

Another synonym for *Stufe*, which further helps to define Schleiermacher's view of the periodization of states of consciousness, is the term *Gebiet*, by which he also designates a definite realm, or sphere, of the conscious development, in contrast to those before and after. In whatever *Gebiet* one finds oneself, one is inevitably aware that it is a limited and distinctive realm of consciousness, and can only be characterized relative to the other realms that are temporally juxtaposed to it. Although the spatial imagery of *Gebiet* is somewhat different when applied

---

[13] Ibid., #29,3.

[14] Ibid., #89,3.

[15] Ibid., #108,6.

[16] Ibid., #29,1.

[17] Ibid., #67,1.

to consciousness than is the temporal imagery of *Zeit* and *Stufe*, Schleiermacher uses it apparently to emphasize that many successive actual moments go into composing a "state" of consciousness, which then is recognized in the larger train of conscious succession as but one "realm" among others.

One may "dwell" in a "realm" of consciousness, but the spatial imagery must be supplemented by the temporal imagery that also characterizes the finitude of existence, so that one "passes" along from one realm to another. Thus we may exist in the realm of sin or of redemption, or one of their variants,[18] but we always have a sense of temporal movement and succession among them as well.

The "stages" of actual self-consciousness, whether called *Zeiten*, *Stufen*, or *Gebiete*, are thus seen by Schleiermacher as the correlatively successive "states" of a life of self-consciousness. The "states" are in reality what develop periodically throughout the course of actually self-conscious life, but when the states are viewed in interrelated succession, they are then able to be called "stages," and are seen to have a kind of developmental or cumulative effect upon one another. But whether talking about a given state or stage, Schleiermacher always has us to remember that they are but composites of the particular actual moments, and that it is the ongoing process of momentary self-actualization which so forms itself into the various states and stages that give to life its developmental character.

The Processing of States into Stages of Actual Self-Consciousness

When we reflect upon the life of self-consciousness, according to Schleiermacher, we are primarily aware of the actual moment of our present existence, but the nature of processing time means that we cannot but also be aware of the succession of moments to which the present one belongs. The context of the moments before and after our present is what enables us to comprehend a stronger sense of the meaning of the actual present, and this context is what we take to be our state, or condition—at the moment, but also surrounding the moment.

---

[18]Ibid., #111,3, #30,1, and #66,2.

The sense of being in a certain state of actual self-consciousness is the sense that one's *existenziell* moments are predominantly actualizing one of the two *existenzial* potencies over the other. A state is therefore the basic drift of a succession of moments, which must inevitably mean that one of the two potentials has gained ascendancy, or power (*Kraftigkeit*)[19] over the other.

This ascendancy may not be altogether continuous, however, because the actualizing self may at any given moment freely shift toward enabling the empowerment of the other potential. But the basic pattern of actually self-conscious life is that one potential will attain a preponderance (*Übergewicht*)[20] of successive momentary actualizations over the other, and thereby establish a basic "state" of existence.

Such a preponderance of moments dominated by a certain potency is both a quantitative accumulation *through* time and a qualitative conditioning *of* time, which together determine the *Zeit*, or stage, of personal existence. This preponderance, or pre-eminence (*Vorrang*),[21] of one potency, moreover, will mean that the other potency must occur in a position of subservience (*gehorsam Sein*)[22] or subjugation (*Unterwerfung*)[23] to it. Even though both *are* present as structural potencies to be conjointly actualized, the reciprocal structure of the actualizing process is such that one must always be realized as more viable than the other.

The ontological overtones of this seemingly inevitable process in existence are such that Schleiermacher can even use the terms "being" and "not-being" to refer to the relative degree of actualization of one potency when compared to the

---

[19]Ibid., #80,3.

[20]Ibid., #29,1.

[21]Ibid., #71,3.

[22]Ibid., #74,1.

[23]Ibid., #89,3.

other. "Every finite state is a blending of being [*Sein*] and not-being [*Nichtsein*],"[24] of the relatively preponderant being of one potency, and of the relatively subservient not-being of the other. Such a "not-being" refers only to the strength of a potency *within* existence, however, usually to the relatively lesser degree of actualization of the always-present God-consciousness, and could in no way be extended, as Barth does, to imply a dualistic "nothingness" into which one's entire existence might fall.

A given state may certainly waver in "degrees of more or less" dominance by a strongly resistant potency, but it will nonetheless demonstrate a predominant drift, or quantitative habituation, in its favor.

> Resistance as an activity by which an opposed activity is to be neutralized, has naturally its degrees of more and less, and is thus an intensive phenomenon conditioned by time, and when present in anything that has life advances by repetition in time to proficiency.[25]

The "resistance" that Schleiermacher refers to here is that of the world-conscious potential asserting itself over the God-consciousness. By the same token, however, the God-consciousness may in its own time attain to dominance, and establish its own preponderant state of existence.[26]

> The activity of the spirit . . . in its effort to win dominion over the flesh, is likewise an intensive power, and as a living force, attains by repetition in time to proficiency.[27]

---

[24]Ibid., #81,1.

[25]Ibid., #67,2.

[26]In his theological perspective, Schleiermacher calls the God-consciousness, "spirit," and he calls the world-consciousness, "flesh." While he basically uses the terms "God-consciousness" and "world-consciousness" in his more presuppositional presentation of a philosophy of religion, he comes to equate them with the powers of spirit and flesh when viewed theologically from a state of piety.

[27]Ibid., #67,2.

Schleiermacher seems to indicate by such passages that every moment of actual self-consciousness is capable in principle of actualizing either of the ingressing potencies, but that in fact the train of successive moments usually tends to have one certain potency dominating the other "more or less" continuously. The longer the period of conditioning, of "repetition in time to proficiency" (*Wiederholung in der Zeit zur Fertigkeit*), the more difficult it becomes for the recessive potency to be empowered over the dominant one.

In spite of the strength of one potency in continuing its state of dominance, every moment in that state will still involve an actual sense of the presence of the subjugated one. There is no moment in even the most "conditioned" state which does not therefore look backward to a time when the other potential was stronger, and also forward to a time when the other may possibly assert its potency again.

The longer-range knowledge of our experiential history does indeed confirm what every moment suggests: our lives involve a succession of *states* that can look backward and forward to one another as contrasting *stages*. Schleiermacher emphasizes over and over in this regard that even in the most intransigent state of sinful dominance by the world-consciousness, the God-consciousness is still fully and characteristically present, as it struggles toward its own time of fulfillment.

By the same token, however, when the God-feeling is in the ascendancy, it too is ever conscious of the insistent presence of world-feeling, as pressing upon both its past and its future:

> In every religious moment the feeling of absolute dependence occurs only as a relative turning away from God or turning towards him.[28]

This view of the impossibility of a perfectly continuous harmony between the two potencies within the entire range of human existence is confirmed not only by

---

[28] Ibid., #62,3.

actual theological insight, but also by the general religio-philosophical outlook of the *Dialectic*:

> The religious feeling, to be sure, is an actually consummated feeling, but it is never pure, for in it the consciousness of God is always tied to that of something else.[29]

The Antithesis of Pleasure and Pain in Every Moment of Actual Self-Consciousness

Because every moment of actual self-consciousness is the outcome of a contest for dominance between two potential powers, its consummation, or conjunction, will involve a sense of success for the one and a sense of defeat for the other. This ambiguous atmosphere is always to be expected in any moment of existence, simply because the two potencies are never to be found in a state of perfect harmony, but will always bear the marks of their unending struggle for dominant realization. The actual moments in which the struggle is continually manifested will therefore involve a two-sided atmosphere, with an aura of pleasure (*Lust*) contributed by the dominant power, and an aura of pain (*Unlust*) contributed by the subservient one.

Are "pleasure" and "pain" seen by Schleiermacher as emotional extrusions to actual moments, or rather as reflective rationalizations upon them? Neither of these interpretations seems really adequate in light of Schleiermacher's understanding of basic "feeling moments," as compared with either "emotions" or "rationalizations." Every "actual moment of feeling" seems rather to *contain* the antithesis of pleasure and pain within it, simply as the formal manner (*wie*) of the conjoined actualizing of two antithetical powers.

---

[29]Schleiermacher, *Dialektik*, (Jonas) 152.

> The antithesis of pleasure and pain refers to the manner in which the two grades of self-consciousness are related to each other in the unity of the moment.[30]

Every unified or conjunctive moment reveals its ambivalent origin from the two impulsing potencies, in that it manifests an aura of pleasure from the one, along with an aura of pain from the other. Since all moments are further involved in a whence and a thence, the pleasure-pain antithesis will also evince the evaluative tendency of discerning whether the respective potencies are more on the wax or on the wane. This sense of vectoral evaluation means that pleasure and pain reflect not only the relative power structure in a given moment, but that they also are sensitive to the long-range tendency of the powers toward dominance or subservience.[31] If the actual self-consciousness is moving in even the slightest direction toward a shift in emphasis between the two powers, the manner, or accent (*Ton*),[32] of the actualization will involve more pleasure on one side and more pain on the other.

Pleasure and pain thus refer to the intrinsic tone, or manner of actualization, within a *moment* of feeling, and within that role they also reflect the vectoral tendency of the *state* in which that moment falls. As intrinsic attributes of the life of feeling, they would therefore participate in the state of feeling *per se*, and could not for Schleiermacher be considered as reflective or conceptual constructs applied to the moments of subjective consciousness by a more objective level of consciousness. The view that Schleiermacher uses "pain" and "pleasure" to designate some such reflective "apprehensions" of the originally subjective

---

[30]Schleiermacher, *The Christian Faith*, #5,4.

[31]Ibid., #62,1.

[32]Ibid., #8,2.

feelings is taken in the study by G. N. Boyd.³³ This view would seem unjustified, however, in light of the many passages in which pain and pleasure are vectoral attributes of the conjoining potencies precisely as they form the fundamental moments of subjective consciousness.

The basic point for Schleiermacher is that the antithetical polarity of pleasure and pain is "the general *form* of *self*-consciousness," that is, the manner of the potencies' coming together to form the "actual content of a moment of experience."³⁴ Every moment of every existence will therefore have a relative degree of both pleasure and pain, depending upon which potency has registered a gain in strength and which has suffered a loss—whether the actualization is a relative "turning toward" (*Hingewendetsein*) or "turning away from" (*Abgewendetsein*) each potency.³⁵ In a moment of dominance by the sensuous consciousness, for instance, "the sensuous self-consciousness, by reason of its having been gratified, is affected with pleasure, but the higher, owing to the impotence of the God-consciousness, with pain."³⁶

The contrasting tendency toward subservience, of course, may also befall the world-consciousness, so that in the long range its moments may involve "either pleasure or pain, according to whether its life is furthered or hindered."³⁷ By the same token, the God-consciousness will experience its dominance as pleasure, or joy, and its diminution as pain, or sorrow:

> Particular actions [even of the pious sort] show in their execution more or less sin, and so do particular purposes. The actual individual self-

---

³³Boyd, "The Doctrine of Original Sin and the Fall in the Theology of Friedrich Schleiermacher," 53, 64-66.

³⁴Schleiermacher, *The Christian Faith*, #62, int.

³⁵Ibid., #62,3.

³⁶Ibid., #66,1.

³⁷Ibid., #5,4.

> consciousness [in a general state of piety] bears witness to this in many a moment of sorrow [pain of the world-consciousness] where the sorrow is assuaged by the simultaneous presence of the constant factor [pleasure of the God-consciousness]. At other moments the [Godly] self-consciousness is a joy that passes into humility because its only right to exist is found in what assuages the sorrow lying so near it.[38]

Schleiermacher seems to be saying in this passage, and in many others that deal with the "final" stage of piety in human existence, that ambiguity and struggle within existence will never be completely resolved. Even within the state of redemption, when the God-consciousness is especially "imparted" and "empowered" to dominance within us, the world-consciousness will never be completely attuned to, or harmonized with it. The "joy" that describes the pleasure of the God-consciousness even then will continue to be antithetically stimulated by the pain from recurring assertions of world-consciousness.[39] The very history of every individual existence must therefore mean that the passage through states of sin and grace will inevitably accumulate the experiences of the actualizing self, and lend to every new moment the sense of a continuing struggle, marked by the antithesis of pleasure and pain.

The Antithesis of Sin and Grace in the Developing Stages of Actual Self-Consciousness

The antithesis of pleasure and pain has been seen as that which describes the tone, or format, *within* each actual moment. The antithesis of sin and grace will now be seen as that which describes the longer-range ambiguity of the entire process of existence, as the struggle for dominance continues *throughout* the moments, and even *throughout* the states of actual self-consciousness. The latter antithesis derives from the former, just as states and stages derive from moments,

---

[38] Ibid., #110,3.

[39] Ibid., #62,1 and #111,3.

THE STAGES OF DEVELOPMENT IN ACTUAL SELF-CONSCIOUSNESS

so that Schleiermacher sees the ambiguity and struggle *within* each moment as that which determines the overall sense of ambiguity and the overall line of struggle *throughout* the course of the life.

The general antithesis of sin and grace qualifies the whole of life, because the specific moments include the pleasure-pain antithesis as a vectoral indicator of the general states that come before and after. Sin and grace, or bondage and redemption, are thus the two basically possible states into which the actual self-consciousness may fall, since each represents the basic dominance of one potential over the other for a certain time of life. The shift from the state of sin to the state of grace is the pivotal step in the struggle for dominance between the powers, and thereby reveals the two states (*Zustande*) also to have been basic stages (*Stufen*) in the progressive development of that existential struggle.

Although the "actual moments of experience"[40] entail the immediate antithesis of pleasure and pain, they thereby reveal the broader implication that all of life will involve a kind of antithetical progression of states of dominance. It is only from the final stage of "grace," however, that the former stages of "sin" and "original co-determination" can clearly be ascertained, and it is then that the antithetical staging of sin and grace can be seen as the developmental outcome of the original state of harmony.

"Sin" and "grace" are Schleiermacher's theological designations for the states that his philosophical terminology would call "the predominance of world-consciousness" and "the predominance of God-consciousness." The significance of the latter religio-philosophical terminology is that it enables us to comprehend the ontological-existential process of struggling potentials that has preceded the final stage of dominance by God-consciousness, in which the state of grace can be only theologically insightful of itself.[41]

---

[40] Ibid., #62,int.

[41] Ibid., #68,3.

The developing course of life certainly is one that must be seen at the final stage of grace in order to be seen complete—yet it is a course that Schleiermacher suggests can best be plotted through the actuality of its various stages with a more generalized philosophical perspective. Theology can be sure only that grace has at last "overcome" and "abounded," but philosophy must then try "phenomenologically" to describe *all* the developments that have led to the possibility and then to the actuality of grace. Although Schleiermacher often mixes his hermeneutical genres and their respective terminological approaches, especially in *The Christian Faith*, it would seem that his general overview of the developmental process of the actual self-consciousness is framed basically in a philosophy-of-religion approach.

Such a phenomenological reflection on the ontological structure as working into the existential process of self-consciousness is not deliberately carried out by Schleiermacher, but it has been the aim of this study to extrapolate such a model based upon the implicitly philosophical categories that Schleiermacher does so frequently use. It is such a model of the processing structure of consciousness that now allows us to discern the three distinct existential stages in the actualization struggle between the basic structural powers—the stages of 1) original co-actualization, 2) predominance by the worldly power, and 3) final predominance by the Godly power.

The most significant point about the entire process of development of the three stages of existence is that all are indeed definite realities as states of actual self-consciousness, even though the earlier two may be dim or incomprehensible from the final stage of realized piety.[42] Nevertheless, from an overall perspective, it is because of the uniquely given reality of the original state of harmony that the succeeding state of sin seems so awfully real, and it is because of the

---

[42]Ibid., #79,1.

stark reality of sin that the antithetical state of grace succesively assumes its distinctive quality of reality.[43]

The antithesis between the states of sin and grace is therefore possible only because there is first an "original" state of co-equality between the two potentials, which then improperly shifts toward an imbalance in the state of sin, and which must then be shifted back in the final state of grace toward a proper reapportionment. During this process of shifting out of the state of balance into one state of dominance, and then into the other, there is a cumulative development of historical awareness that progressively qualifies the actual self-consciousness as the antithesis of sin and grace. Each successive state is by definition a stage-like progression from the last, although each is also by definition a distinctively qualified manner of actualization applied to the conjoining potencies.

In the state of original co-determination, we explicitly reactualize the implicitly proportionate structure of the two potencies just as they are given, or "posited" to us. In the next stage, we assert our own formalizing impress upon the manner of their conjunction, and so allow the world-consciousness to become dominant over the God-consciousness, in the state of sin.

In the final stage, we find that the imbalance is redressed, and that the God-consciousness gracefully reasserts itself to its proper manner of actualization, even without our deliberate involvement in the process of shifting. At each step of the way, however, we are somehow made to be aware of what has gone before, so that each new style of actualization executes its existential format in light of what has constituted its progress thus far.[44]

From the final stage of grace, therefore, the *God-consciousness* is seen in the previous stage of sin to have been dormant but implicitly graceful, and in the original stage of co-determination to have been powerful only in a proprietary sort of way. From the final stage of grace, in contrast, the *world-consciousness* (then

---

[43]Ibid., #29,1.

[44]Ibid., #63,2 and #63,3.

actualized as a consciousness of defeated sin) is seen in the previous stage of actual sin to have been disproportionately dominant, and in the original stage of co-determination to have been powerful in the uniquely incipient form of original sin.[45]

The stage of grace is thus understood by Schleiermacher to be a radically new state of selfhood (in that the human God-consciousness is empowered from without), even while it is also the only natural outcome of the process of human development (in which sin had blocked the original empowerment of God-consciousness).

> The doctrine of the church postulates the good [original perfection] as immediately produced by God, and, since with the [sinful] loss of this condition the development is broken and a new point of departure is needed [into grace], the redeemer can come in as the turning point.[46]

The natural process of human development is at once "broken" and completed, indicating that the state of grace is both a natural "turning point" from the state of sin and a radically unexpected departure in the manner of its accomplishment. The "antithesis of sin and grace" is therefore to be seen basically as the antithesis of opposing *stages*, but at the same time as an antithesis of opposing *moments*, an antithesis that still manifests itself *within* the state of grace, whenever the tendency to sin may momentarily reassert itself.

The Factors of Determinism and Freedom in the Development of Actual Self-Consciousness

The problem of what even Schleiermacher recognized to be the "antinomy" between determinism and freedom has previously been considered, in regard to the manner in which the formally "free" actualization of self-consciousness transpires

---

[45]Ibid., #69, postscript.

[46]Ibid., #61,5.

to conjoin the materially "determined" potentials of self-consciousness that comprise it. The same problem of how freedom and determination may both be seen as factors in human life must now be considered in regard to the alternating flow of dominant moments in the developing states of actual self-consciousness. The crux of the antinomy is still the same, however, as the question of why a perfectly proportioned structure of self-consciousness should in its actual operation fall into a continuous pattern of disproportionality.

In the precise terms of ontological structure underlying existential process, Schleiermacher tries to maintain that the structurally stable actual self-consciousness somehow becomes unstable in the progressive unfolding of its moments. While the actual self-consciousness as a structural element of self-consciousness is *determined* to be the *free-form* re-establishment of the elemental potencies, somehow its free capacity for re-formulating the essential proportion of the potencies is never able to recapture their original arrangement.

Thus it is that the putative "freedom" of actualization finds itself incorrigibly determined by the powers and the process that it supposes itself to control. Any given moment of actual existence, as an exercise of free intention and formalization of its potentials, still must be seen as determined by the very externality of the two powers that implode upon it, with different existential dynamics than those of the essential level of the self's determination by God and by world. Moreover, the continuing process of development of the successive moments of actualization incurs an accumulation, or conditioning, into the states and stages that further determine the quality of subsequent "free" actualizations.

The actual self-consciousness for Schleiermacher is thus freely "self-actualizing" only in a very limited sense, for the subject's potentials for actualization are determined in the existential incommensurability with which they are received, and by the cumulative pattern of reciprocal tension into which they arrange themselves. The potencies thus present themselves into the actual mode of self-consciousness as agents simply derived from that level of reality that is the *essential* self's complete determination. When they now find themselves to be represented into the self's *existential* level of determination, they are actually operative at a different level of the self's reality, and therefore are thrown into the contest for domination of the existential self-actualization that finally can be mediated only by that free actualization itself.

The antinomy of determinism and freedom is thus manifested in terms of how the complete determination by God and his world of the essential self can be attenuated into the form of free representations of those powers at the level of the existing self. How is it, Schleiermacher must ask in traditional theological terms, that the divinely ordained order of essential selfhood can become disordered when it is allowed to be recapitulated by the also divinely ordained existential self? What is it about the nature of existence, of actual self-consciousness, that both comprehends its basic determination and also freely misrepresents it?

Schleiermacher's answer to this question concerning the antinomy of perfect determination and imperfect freedom would seem to many the starting point of a theodicy. Yet Schleiermacher does often disclaim even the possibility of such a full-blown theoretical explanation of *how* and *why* God allows sin and evil, much less the intention of formulating one. Rather, his effort to explain the antinomy basically stays at a descriptive level of just *what* happens during the course of human existence in the dynamics of determination and freedom.

What "happens" in the course of existence is precisely the dialectical process of the determining potencies' struggle for domination, which is in actuality the substance of human freedom. But this very process of actualizing freedom is seen by Schleiermacher to happen only as a result of divine ordination, which to us involves both means and end.

Even though the existent's actualizing freedom is its most definitive reality, it still will be seen from the overall perspective of implicit determination that freedom is ordained as the "efficient" means to God's absolutely "commanded" end for humankind. We cannot, to be sure, ever understand the absolute terms of God's commanding will—that is, the how and the why—but we can at least describe our experiences, which are what he uses as efficient means to the fulfillment of his will.[47]

The description of every human life that eventually emerges is that of the faltering stages of freedom, as it actualizes its potentials out of the state of primeval perfection, into the state of sin, and finally into the state of redemption. That such as uneven course could be ordained by the divine will is of course incomprehensible to humans, and even at the completion of the course we can never understand how or why God would command it, but only that he could effectively use it to complete his command.

> [Sin] as a want of conformity to the commanding [*gebietend*] will of God can nonetheless be brought about by his efficient [*hervorbringend*] will.[48]

In this sense sin "is grounded in the divine causality," but only under that efficient divine will which grants it the sort of "reality . . . ordained by God as that which makes redemption necessary."[49] The commanding will of God, as his ultimate and complete will, could therefore never ordain sin *per se*, but only with the ultimate effect of redemption.

> By the commanding will, accordingly, sin has been ordained by God, not indeed sin in and of itself, but sin merely in relation to redemption; for otherwise redemption itself could not have been ordained.[50]

Schleiermacher is forced to use the conceptual device of a subsidiary will in the divine determination, which is thus able to operate in and through a human

---

[47]Ibid., #81,1.

[48]Ibid.

[49]Ibid., #81,3.

[50]Ibid.

being's own free will. Such a device is able to mitigate the antinomy of determinism and freedom, although it clearly tilts the resolution toward the side of determinism. The free capacity of human beings to actualize their own existence, and apparently to sin, is conducted only under the aegis of the divine will, effecting an end "greater than all our sin."

> In relation to every finite [and sinful] nature there is an efficient divine will—not, however, as something existing purely by itself, but as contained in the [commanding] will which creates the finite God-consciousness in its entirety, and thus embraces redemption likewise.[51]

Because the efficient will that ordains sin does it on behalf of the "entirety" (*Gesamtheit*) of divine will, in which it is "contained" (*enthalten*), it seems clear that the efficient will as responsible for the track of human freedom is really an operative subsidiary for what the entire divine will cannot perfectly command.

From the standpoint of mankind's final state of redemption, Schleiermacher comes to regard the "efficient will" of God as the only conceptual means available for describing the apparently determined development of human freedom through the state of sin and into the state of grace. The instrumentally "efficient" will of God must be introduced because

> The term redemption is not so suitable to describe the divine decree [commanding] as it is to describe the effect of the decree [efficient], for the almighty cannot ordain one thing [redemption] for the sake of another [sin] which he has not ordained. From this standpoint, no better expression can be found for the divine decree than a Biblical one [creation], which at the same time indicates the effect as a whole.[52]

---

[51]Ibid., #81,1.

[52]Ibid., #89,1.

The complete and commanded decree of God is thus creation as a whole, while the subsidiary and efficient decree, which is not really God's perfectly commanded will, but is utilized toward its fulfillment, is the process of sin-leading-to-redemption. In this sense even sin and redemption come to be seen as the process of "new creation,"[53] which is the means of completing the overall original creation, "the one undivided eternal decree."[54]

That we live our existences out in such a framework, aware that we are both freely active and teleologically determined, is what our phenomenological philosophy of existence tells us, and even the theological reflections from the final stage of piety can only tell us that God was using *those* means to *this* present end. Further speculation as to God's original or final purposes, in terms of why and how God exercises such efficient means, is both impossible and unnecessary.

Schleiermacher insists that our theological speculations must be relatively modest, especially in regard to efforts to explain sin and evil as part of God's comprehensive will. We can only be sure of our phenomenological discoveries that freedom leads to real sin, which is not good, but that it can then lead to real redemption, which is good. The logical antinomy of the two, which is really the antinomy of freedom and determination, also can only be resolved phenomenologically, when we perceive the state of redemption to be the good end toward which we have been determined during the entire process.

In thus dealing with the antinomy in as modest a way as possible, Schleiermacher avoids the sort of full-blown speculative theodicies that tried before him to spin out the logical implications of freedom and determinism on a metaphysical scale. In his Kantian type of reserve, Schleiermacher believes that such transcendental principles are beyond our ken, and that we can only say from our phenomenal standpoint of pious feeling that we are in a *good* world, not necessarily the *best* of all logically possible worlds. We do not know if or how God could have

---

[53]Ibid.

[54]Ibid., #94,3.

made our world better—we only know that God does efficiently bring a redemptive good out of the misfortune of sin.

Schleiermacher seems to suggest that the antinomies of freedom and determination, and of human sin and divine perfection, are in truth confusions of our finite perspective, and should not be projected upon the metaphysical plane of absolute principles. He points out, for instance, how it is better to explain things to ourselves with a phenomenological forbearance than to get lost in the metaphysical contradictions of theodicies such as those of Augustine.

Augustine, as Schleiermacher points out, was variously led on both sides of the antinomies to both optimistic and pessimistic views of the nature of evil.[55] At times he tries to maintain the ultimacy of goodness in God's creation, in such doctrines as the *felix culpa* and the privative view of evil; at other times, however, he tries to maintain the surd presence of evil in creation, as in his doctrines of the radical nature of freedom and of double predestination.

Schleiermacher simply wants to point out that such transcendental logic can never resolve the issues, because humans can never know the entire range of ultimate truth. The freedom and the determination that we know are finitely bound up with the actual developments of sin and grace in our existence, and are only known by inference as part of the universal will of God.

> We must not forget that in thus considering the consciousness of sin *per se* we are moving in the region of the abstract, and should therefore err were we to look for divine activities bearing upon sin purely by itself.[56]

Divine activity can bear upon sin only in the subsidiary manner of what is called God's "efficient will," which is his instrumental intention for using sin for its opposite purpose.

---

[55]Ibid., #72,2 and #72,6.

[56]Ibid., #79,1.

Not even where sin is viewed from the standpoint of a paramount God-consciousness can we conceive of divine attributes that have to do with sin apart from its disappearance as a result of redemption.[57]

The situation in which we are actually able to conceive of what God's will has accomplished through our freedom is that of redemption, but even here we can only conceive of God's relation to sin as that which "disappears as a result of redemption." Schleiermacher does not flinch from saying that God was indeed determinatively present during the state of sin, as is done in such casuistic doctrines as "the permissive will of God" or "the dark side of God's nature." But he does believe that God's determinative ordainment of sin is effected only with a view toward accomplishing the perfect, or commanded, will of God in redemption.

Our conception of the total working of God's efficient and commanding will is derived from what we perceive as the *antithesis* of sin and grace, because in the course of our experience the former is opposite to the latter, even though it is its necessary reciprocal. The antinomy that we perceive between our freedom in sin and God's determination in grace is able to be resolved within the phenomenal context of our state of grace, but only inasmuch as we experience redemption through Christ. Only Christ can demonstrate how divine determination and human freedom are ultimately consonant and not antithetical, because only he freely bears the determination of our sin, and opens our freedom to the determination of God's grace.[58]

Reflections on the Stages of Existence as Carried Out by Philosophy and Theology

Our reflective examination of the developing states of actual self-consciousness is carried out in a comprehensive way by the approach of philosophy,

---

[57]Ibid., #64,2.

[58]Ibid., #104,2.

which for Schleiermacher focuses on the developmental process of *all* the states, as they seem inexorably to pass from one to another. Our reflection on the *single* state of piety, however, is carried out in a more specific way by the approach of theology, which perceives even the "human" state of piety as being under a special determination of divine empowerment. Much of what Schleiermacher has to say about the *general* pattern of development of the states, however, seems informed by what he knows only in reference to the *specific* state of piety; therefore many of his "philosophical" reflections seem so aware of the Godly involvement in the development of all the states that they should probably be taken to constitute a "philosophy of religion."

Most of the categories that we will now designate as the "stages of development in actual self-consciousness" probably would fall in Schleiermacher's estimation under some such hybrid approach to reflection. Since he would be most careful to insist that properly "theological" concepts have to do exclusively with actually pious moments in the state of dominant God-consciousness, he would probably allow that reflections on the other developing states, including those which allude to the incipient stage of the God-consciousness, are framed more in a "philosophical" approach. It is to establish this basic hermeneutical assessment of Schleiermacher's methodology that we now try to delineate the philosophical categories with which he traces the development of the specific power of piety through the general stages of consciousness.

The philosophy-of-religion approach now to be followed is no longer an ontological-philosophy, as in the previous examination of the structure of consciousness, but is instead an existential-philosophy, which categorizes the existing actual moments in their processing states of consciousness. (This divergence of emphases in philosophy is to be noted in what the ontologically oriented *Dialectic* says about the very kind of existential-philosophy followed in *The Christian Faith*.)[59]

---

[59]Schleiermacher, *Dialektik*, (Jonas) 129.

In *The Christian Faith* Schleiermacher thus looks back at his preliminary discussions of the structure of consciousness and calls them philosophical "presuppositions" to the theological propositions of the actual state of piety.

> We shall exhaust the whole compass of Christian doctrine if we consider the facts of the religious self-consciousness, first, as they are *presupposed* by the antithesis [of sin and grace], and secondly, as they are *determined* by that antithesis.[60]

Somewhere in between the ontological-philosophical "presuppositions" and the existential-theological "antithesis" of sin and grace must have arisen Schleiermacher's existential-philosophical philosophy-of-religion reflections on how the structure unfolds itself into the antithesis.

ORIGINAL CO-DETERMINATION BY WORLD-CONSCIOUSNESS AND GOD-CONSCIOUSNESS

The Co-Existence of the Potencies in a Primeval State

The first stage in the developing life of actual self-consciousness is considered by Schleiermacher to be *primeval* in two senses: it is the quantitative basis for the others, their implicit genetic origin, and it is also a normative state of qualitative perfection, unaffected by the later antithesis of sin and grace. And yet, because its sense of innate perfection is infused by the sense of implicit developmental dislocation, Schleiermacher has difficulty in portraying the actual nature of such an "original" state. For this reason, it appears that to call such a vaguely apprehended time of life an actual "state" may be a misapplication of the term, as it is typically used by Schleiermacher to refer to the fully manifest states of actual development in self-consciousness.

---

[60]Schleiermacher, *The Christian Faith*, #29, int.

The originative period of life is probably best seen as a stage (*Stufe*), in the sense of a temporally preliminary time of life that stands before the other stages, whether or not it can justifiably be called an actual state (*Zustand*), in which one potency is more determinative than the other. Schleiermacher recognizes this situation when he calls it a "preliminary condition,"[61] which is only a "part condition"[62] of the fully fledged actual states to come. The potencies are both present, but neither has become dominant enough fully to engender an "actual state," so they remain in a not fully actualized situation that is "anterior" to the subsequently developing states of existence. With the potencies hanging in a state of preliminary separation, with neither in actual control, Schleiermacher thus believes that such a state is at best "incomplete" (*unvollständig*)[63] and at worst to be acknowledged as a state of confusion (*Verworrenheit*).[64]

This characterization of the primal stage in life as incomplete and confused is made, however, only from the later stages of insight, which see the explicit antitheses of existence as simply uncertain and implicit at the beginning. Exactly how and why the two incipient potencies are primevally posited with their tendencies to alternating states of actual dominance we will never know. We can define the primeval state only "abstractly,"[65] even in light of the empirical certainty that it was there as the temporal origin of all that has succeeded it.

That of which we *can* be sure is that the primal state had a formal balance (co-determination) between the two incipient potencies, even though their material differences were also present. We can simply deduce that in this "state" there was as yet no actualization process fully to characterize an existent self-consciousness,

---

[61] Ibid., #67,1.

[62] Ibid., #69, postscript.

[63] Ibid., #6,1.

[64] Ibid., #6,1, #5,3, and #5,1.

[65] Ibid., #79,1 and #61,5.

THE STAGES OF DEVELOPMENT IN ACTUAL SELF-CONSCIOUSNESS 127

which leads Schleiermacher to say that such a preliminary time before existence was necessarily incomplete. Since the potencies were not yet in process of actualization, neither of them could be self-assertively dominant, and we therefore must logically believe them to have been in a state of balance, or co-ordination.

In this way Schleiermacher comes to portray the earliest "state" as one of co-existence (*Zusammensein*),[66] in which the potencies are determined as co-posited (*mitgegeben*)[67] with one another. That both of them are thus fully present, as real potentials for all subsequent states of existence—regardless of their contrary styles of domination—is clearly asserted by Schleiermacher in his formula that they are "equally inherent" (*ebenfalls anerschaffen*)[68] in the original stage.

If the potentials are found to be formally equal in their primal setting, how is it that they also can be found even then to have incipient tendencies toward alternating disequilibrium in the actual forms of later existence? How is it, as a result, that Schleiermacher can find the same primeval state to be determined both by basic goodness and by relative badness?

> We distinguish between our good nature—for many impulses even of sense do not seek to pass beyond what the spirit itself demands of them—and our evil nature, and we are conscious of each of these as something got and received by us conjointly with others.[69]

What indeed constitutes our good nature and our evil nature, especially at the preliminary stage of human existence, where neither is yet actualized?

---

[66]Ibid., #72,6.

[67]Ibid.

[68]Ibid., #72,5.

[69]Ibid., #69,1.

Certainly the "good" and the "evil" natures in us are *not* to be equated with the God-consciousness and the world-consciousness *per se*, in any sort of fundamental dualism. The whole ontology of existence that Schleiermacher presupposes disallows such an outlook, and rather suggests that it is the actualized manner of their meeting which constitutes the good and the evil aspects of existence. It is the tendency (*Hinneigung, Leichtigkeit*)[70] toward dominant actualization which each potency has ingrained within it which constitutes the origination of good, in the case of God-consciousness, and the origination of evil, in the case of world-consciousness. Yet each "tendency" in this primeval stage is only "part" of a condition of existence, and cannot lead to an actual moment or actual state of dominance except in the fully conjunctive stages, in which both potencies are reciprocally involved.

It is only in remembering that the potencies have both material potential *and* dynamic powers that we can comprehend how they may in the primordial "state" be regarded as "tendencies" for the domination of a completely actualized state. It is therefore in this regard that we must now examine each primeval potency in turn, to discern just what about its material content and dynamic thrust make it likely or unlikely to achieve dominance in the subsequently developing stages of existence.

The Tendency toward Domination by World-Consciousness as Original Sin

There seems to be no question for Schleiermacher that the worldconsciousness should and would be an entirely good component of existence, if it were able to be actualized in existence in the same formal alignment with God-consciousness as obtains in their essential proportionality. But because the world-consciousness is now to be a reciprocal potency for the self's existence, rather than a determinant of the self's essence, it will be able not only to be actualized, but to be actualized

---

[70]Ibid., #72,2.

in a form of disproportionate dominance that it does not enjoy at the level of essence.

The very context of existence-as-actualization therefore involves the world-consciousness being placed in a capacity for self-potentiation that carries with it the actual power of becoming dominant. It is just this given (*gesetzt*) situation of empowerment which constitutes the drive or tendency to gain dominant actualization in consciousness, and it is this tendency which Schleiermacher calls original sin (*Erbsünde*).

The "tendency toward sin" (*Hinneigung zur Sünde*)[71] is termed original because it is found by every individual as the manner or form in which a person's world-consciousness is initially received. In likeness to the figuratively original people, Adam and Eve, we also find ourselves with

> a sinfulness already present, since misuse of the [actualizing] free will by itself is no explanation, but forces us to assume something else as prompting it . . . something already present in the soul which implied a certain readiness [*Leichtigkeit*] to pass into [dominant] sensuous appetite.[72]

The tendency, or readiness, for world-consciousness to become dominant seems implicitly presented to us "to develop without having the God-consciousness directed upon [it] in its initial stages."[73] The overpoweringness of the tendency suggests that it is "something received" (*ein Empfangenes*),[74] an "inherent quality" of the potentiating self, which one can only acknowledge as

---

[71]Ibid.

[72]Ibid.

[73]Ibid., #67,1.

[74]Ibid., #71,1 and #69, postscript.

"congenital" (*mitgebornen*).[75] Schleiermacher uses further Biblical imagery to denote that quality of the world-consciousness by which it is "bent" on dominance, and so categorizes it as the "flesh," which will subsequently struggle against the "spirit," or the drive for dominance by God-consciousness.

> If our God-consciousness is not yet developed, there can be no resistance to it, but merely an independent activity of the flesh which, though in time it will quite naturally come to act as a resistance to the spirit, cannot at that stage be regarded as sin in the proper sense, but rather as the germ of sin.[76]

At the original stage of co-determination, the potencies are still in preliminary form, "independent" of one another and thus able to gauge their full potential only in reference to their future contest for dominant actualization. The "tendency" of the world-consciousness at this preliminary stage is thus only a foreshadowing of its dominant actualization as "flesh," and this is why Schleiermacher says the tendency must be considered sinful not actually, but only originally, as the "germ of sin" (*Keim der Sünde*).

The propositions thus far presented would seem to suggest that Schleiermacher saw the original state of world-consciousness as powerfully, positedly, and innately "tending" toward the actualization of sin—but the question might still remain of whether it would *inevitably* develop into sin. In the theological purview of the complete divine determination of the course of life, the answer has already clearly been established in the affirmative. But in the more gradual philosophical approach, with a phenomenological examination of each stage of existence, the answer to the question of inevitability can only be given in terms that describe the operational aspects of determination.

---

[75] Ibid., #71,1.

[76] Ibid., #67,1.

What is it, then, about the phenomenal unfolding of the original state of world-consciousness that explicitly indicates that its tendency toward domination will in fact be actualized as sin? Schleiermacher describes the situation as

> a timeless original sinfulness always and everywhere inhering in human nature and co-existing with the original perfection given along with it—though in such a way that from the concomitance and development of the two there could issue no active righteousness properly so-called, but at best a vacillation between vitiated spiritual efforts and increasing and fully matured sin.[77]

The original sinfulness, although apparently "co-existing" with the original perfection, yet "exists in such a way" that *its* tendency to actual sin will inevitably overcome the tendency toward actual perfection. What is this "way," in which the world-consciousness has its tendency to dominance, which the God-consciousness has not, and which therefore originally posits humankind in a "complete incapacity for good?"[78]

The unique "way" in which the world-conscious tendency for domination is capacitated involves its linkage to the objective presence of the world, which serves as a ready and quick "incentive" for the subjective feelings of world potency. As in the primordial Eve, so also in everyone else we find

> a clear representation of the independent activity and revolt of the sensuous element that develops so readily upon any external incentive by way of opposition to a divine command, and likewise a clear view of how there comes to be conjoined therewith an all too easily effected vitiation of the already developed God-consciousness.[79]

---

[77]Ibid., #72,6.

[78]Ibid., #70, int.

[79]Ibid., #72,5.

Before we further consider just *how* this contact with the external world inevitably drives the inward world-consciousness to actualize its tendency for dominance, we should first consider how the original God-consciousness asserts its own real, but unsuccessful, bid for dominance against the eventually stronger world-potency.

The Tendency toward Domination by God-Consciousness as Original Perfection

Because Schleiermacher regards the two potencies for consciousness as being formally equal in their capacities for determining actual moments and states, he both logically and empirically finds that the God-consciousness has the same kind of innate "tendency" (*Richtung, Hinneigung*) toward domination as does the world-consciousness. Even though its strength will be found greater in the long-run than in the short-run of life, it is nonetheless reckoned in the original stage to be posited equally with its own natural drive for fulfillment.

> In the knowledge of the elements of this *original* perfection as *present in everyone* we find a justification for the original demand that the God-consciousness should exist *continuously* and *universally*.[80]

The disposition toward actualizing the God-consciousness is found so continuously and universally throughout all stages of human life that it must logically be inferred to have been part of the original human endowment. Nonetheless, the certainty of its having been originally determined by God is ultimately known only by the faith that discerns and characterizes God-consciousness throughout its process of development.

> To understand the fundamental aspects of human life as set forth in the above description of man's original perfection, i.e., so that everything is related to the God-consciousness, is, undoubtedly a matter of faith.[81]

---

[80]Ibid., #60,3 (emphasis mine).

[81]Ibid., #61,1.

What faith comes to believe and what existential philosophy implies is that original perfection involves both the tendency toward God-consciousness and the real capacity for having it actualized, ultimately throughout the human race:

> The predisposition to God-consciousness, as an inner impulse, includes the consciousness of a faculty of attaining, by means of the human organism, to those states of self-consciousness in which the God-consciousness can realize itself, and the impulse inseparable therefrom to express the God-consciousness includes in like manner the connection of the race-consciousness with the personal consciousness; and both together form man's original perfection.[82]

Original perfection is not, therefore, a logically primordial capacity that is only hypothetically possible; it is rather a fully potential drive that is actually present in every given moment of existence:

> We account it part of the original perfection of man that in our clear and waking life a continuous God-consciousness as such is possible; and on the contrary, we should have to regard it as an essential imperfection if the emergence of the feeling of absolute dependence, though not abrogating any feeling of partial dependence or freedom, were confined as such to separate and scattered moments.[83]

Obviously Schleiermacher believes that the God-consciousness does not "abrogate" the world-consciousness (any feeling of partial dependence or freedom) but that the two are formally equal in their capacities for actual dominance. Furthermore, he also believes that the primeval period of original co-existence involves within itself a temporal frame of development, in which the power of world-consciousness is "more or less" early in its appearance compared with the power of God-consciousness.

---

[82] Ibid., #60, int.

[83] Ibid., #60,1.

At the climax of the primeval period, to be sure, both potencies are fully manifesting their urges for dominance in a co-existent, coeval manner. But it seems that the objectively sensible reference of the world-consciousness is what leads it first into the full realization of its tendency, which is original sin, as precedent to the God-consciousness' realization of its tendency, which is original perfection.

> For it is only in connexion with his [sense] organs that man realizes sovereignty over the world, of which he can only be conscious as something based upon the divine omnipotence; and it is only inasmuch as the simple activity of spirit is expressed through the medium of space and time that it awakens, as a copy thereof, the consciousness of a divine causality.[84]

God-consciousness is always an incipient potency, from the first moment of life, but it becomes fully formed, as a tendency toward domination of life, only in sequence with the developing world-consciousness. It seems to Schleiermacher to be the "law of mortal existence"[85] that humans first feel their relative dependence upon the world, before they can feel their joint dependence along with the world upon the absolute source of both. From the ontological perspective, both potencies must be seen as co-eval and co-equal, yet Schleiermacher recognizes empirically that the world-consciousness is somehow posited as temporally and spatially antecedent.

> The disposition to the God-consciousness can be represented as a continuous impartation of that consciousness, but only in a degree that is infinitely small; with the consequence that the transition to a definite and perceptible magnitude is always dependent on some other fact of consciousness. . . . Clearly our religious consciousness is not such that

---

[84]Ibid., #59,2.

[85]Ibid., #89,3.

more and less do not apply to it; on the contrary, it oscillates between these extremes, sharing, as it does, the variations of our temporal life.[86]

Although original sin as the strength of the world-consciousness shows a quicker tendency toward development, the original perfection of the God-consciousness must also develop apace within the preliminary stage of existence before either of them can attain to dominance in the fully manifest stages of actual consciousness. It is clear, therefore, that original sin can have no bearing in actual life except as it is joined by original perfection as the co-equal but countervalent tendency, which original sin must then overcome in order to establish the first actual stage in life, the state of "actual sin."

> The [actual] state of sin over its entire range actually presupposes the original perfection of man, and is indeed dependent on it.
> [Actual] sin manifests itself only in connection with and by means of already existent [original] good, and what it obstructs is future good.[87]

Schleiermacher seems to be saying that the first actual sin could occur only when the original tendency to sin had conjoined, and overcome, the fully developed original tendency to good.

> The statement that man was created by God good, righteous, and holy, means that . . . the [original] real state of man could not have been one of sin. For [actual] sin must have been preceded by knowledge and recognition of the divine will, and in that case it must have been preceded by free activity which was not sinful.[88]

Original perfection, even though it is overcome by original sin, is still held by Schleiermacher to be a real and viable potency for actualization, which will in

---

[86] Ibid., #62,1.

[87] Ibid., #68,2.

[88] Ibid., #61,5.

truth be found to be the greater power in the ultimate course of our development. "Original perfection" says Schleiermacher, "expresses the unity of our development, so sin in turn represents its intermittent and disjointed character."[89] Original sin cannot represent a radical sense of "fall," or cleavage, in God's overall determination, because it would thus imply

> that the original perfection of the world has not remained the same, [and would fail] to mention the unity of the whole world-order in its relation to the creation and the continuity of the divine preservation.[90]

Original sin is for Schleiermacher a real potential of dominant actualization, but original perfection is just as real, and represents the ultimate goal of development, because it reflects the underlying pattern of our essential selves, the "unity" and "continuity" which God ordains for every human personality.

> Since the entire course of time can only be an unbroken activity of the whole original perfection, the final result must be an absolute satisfaction, and similarly each moment, taken in the whole, satisfactory as an approximation.[91]

Original perfection is indeed the "unbroken activity" of God-consciousness striving for its proper dominance, and its ultimate success is no more a coincidental matter of fortunate development than is the initial unfortunate development of actual sin a coincidence. Rather, the actualization of the original perfection is able to be effected only in the renewing perfection of Christ:

---

[89]Ibid., #68,2.

[90]Ibid., #59, postscript.

[91]Ibid.

> If we are to see everything that can develop out of such original perfection all together in a single human instance, it is not to be sought in Adam, in whom it must have again been lost, but in Christ, in whom it has brought gain to all.[92]

The final actualization of God-consciousness could not be empowered by Christ, on the other hand, unless it were throughout the "developing course of time" the real potential that we see given in the beginning as "original perfection." In reference to typical theological formulations, Schleiermacher wants to "acknowledge with Augustine that some element of the original good must still survive in human nature,"[93] so that the original sinfulness of being "not able not to sin" will have a basis for eventually being overcome. In order to comprehend just what Christ's redemption accomplishes, Schleiermacher says we must realize that it is the graceful renewal of that original divine empowerment which seemed to be hopelessly obscured by the state of sin:

> We must not magnify our congenital sinfulness to such an extent as would involve the denial of man's capacity to appropriate redemption, for that capacity is the very least that can be predicated of that disposition to the God-consciousness which is inherent in man's original perfection.[94]

Original perfection, as the inherent human "disposition to the God-consciousness," is given to humans as co-equal in power with the disposition to world-consciousness, but human beings find it further given to them that the world-consciousness is determined to fulfill its tendency earlier while leaving the God-consciousness to a later fulfillment. The God-consciousness in the end will be seen to have been a constituent component of every stage of life, but to have necessarily been the dominant component only in the climactic stage of redemption.

---

[92]Ibid., #61,5.

[93]Ibid., #70,2.

[94]Ibid.

> This desire for fellowship with God, never entirely extinguished, though pushed back to the very frontiers of consciousness, [is] part of the original perfection of human nature. This desire [for fulfillment of the power of God-consciousness] is simply the ineradicable residuum in human nature of the original impartation of the divine which makes human nature what it is.[95]

Humans find the God-consciousness as a given part of their nature, but they find that it is given not only originally, but also developmentally, as the highest potential in the enduring process of creation and recreation of that nature.

The Co-equality of Original Sin and Original Perfection Becoming Actually Tilted Toward Sin

If original sin and original perfection are found in the preliminary "stage" of life to be co-equally posited, or inherent, in human nature, it seems in Schleiermacher's ontological reasoning to be because both of them are still only potencies *tending* toward actualization, with neither of them yet actualized in a "state" of dominance over the other. When finally both potencies are fully empowered tendencies, the contest is joined, and the fully actualized states of existence begin.

Even though it is the definitive role of human freedom thus to actualize the formal meeting of the two potentials, the fully actualizing self nevertheless becomes impelled by a greater necessity, to accede first to the domination of world-consciousness. It is this step that launches the first real state of human existence—the state of actual sin—with domination by the world-consciousness and subservience in the God-consciousness.

The step into such fully actualized, self-conscious moments of life is able to occur, however, only because the God-consciousness has become a fully viable

---

[95]Ibid., #108,6.

potential in distinct countervalence to the more entrenched power of world-consciousness.

> It is only when the God-consciousness has been attained that we acknowledge its preeminence among the elements of consciousness and strive for its supremacy; and when this takes place, the antagonism of flesh, as a permanent factor determinative of the actuality of individual sins, must also become a fact of consciousness.[96]

Even though flesh thereby becomes the dominant power in the beginning, still there is the "residuum" of insight that the power of the spirit has a more ultimate goal:

> We can now see the appropriateness of linking the first consciousness of sin, due to the accession of the God-consciousness, with the first presentiment of redemption.[97]

Schleiermacher wants to maintain the sense of human freedom in this joining together of the two potential powers, even while he recognizes them to proceed from determinative sources beyond the actualizing role of free self-consciousness.

> The sinful self-assertiveness of sense, proceeding as it does from its earliest development, has a more remote source than the individual's own life. But once the God-consciousness has emerged as a definite and effective power (*wirksame Grösse*), and as capable of growth, then every moment in which it does not actualize itself as such . . . is an arrest upon the higher activity—an arrest originating in the doer himself—and is a veritable sin.[98]

---

[96] Ibid., #71,3.

[97] Ibid.

[98] Ibid., #69,3.

When the God-consciousness has fully emerged as the capacity for original perfection, its actualization in reference to the world-consciousness then becomes a matter of whether the individual can freely follow through in his or her existential responsibility. This first turning point in life, in which people become somehow responsible for actualizing the pattern of their own existence is roughly what Schleiermacher would acknowledge as an "age of accountability."

> The more thoroughly we trace back the state of our spiritual life to a conscious beginning, to a general "taking command of one's self," which is represented in every decision of the will, the more we are conscious of [original] sin even preceding that.[99]

Even though the power of world-consciousness precedes the advent of our responsibility, we become perfectly clear as to what God-consciousness requires after its co-presence presents us with the mandate to choose.

> The taking command of one's self is simply the discernment of the absolute superiority of those [sensible] states of mind which combine with the God-consciousness without obstructing it.[100]

At the time of actually taking charge of our lives, however, the sense of freedom is still suffused by the sense of determination, and the tendency toward actualization of world-consciousness becomes to everyone irresistibly strong. We sense that we are freely trying to balance both world and God as determinants of our conscious existence, but we then also sense the determinatively "unfree" impulse of the world moving to aggrandize itself into domination of all free moments. The historical accidentality of existential freedom comes to us underlain by a natural inevitability of ontological determination. In anticipation of Kierkegaard's fully explicated paradox, Schleiermacher points out the antinomy

---

[99]Ibid., #67,2.

[100]Ibid., #68,1.

of our involvement in a finitely good world becoming a blockage to our involvement with the infinitely good divine.

But without going any further into metaphysical speculation as to the nature and origin of the antinomy, Schleiermacher remains more content than most theologians in simply providing a basically philosophical description of how the antinomy is experienced in the course of human existence. How it happens is thus explained in the phenomenology of the original shift toward dominance by world-consciousness over God-consciousness, in which the phenomenal human freedom of self-actualization experiences an extra-phenomenal inevitability induced from beyond the self.

How it is that this tendency toward actualization of world-consciousness is effected is what Schleiermacher relates in his discussion of the spatial externality and temporal anteriority of the physical world, as it provides the "incentive" to world-consciousness which makes it so primordially strong. The phenomenological examination of early life points to the *objectivity* of the outside world as a kind of link or trigger, which facilitates the early tendency toward dominance in the *subjective* consciousness of the world. This "revolt of the sensuous element that develops so readily upon any external incentive"[101] is examined by Schleiermacher to the same extent that any phenomenon of the conscious life may be, but the ultimate questions of why and for what purpose it so happens are questions that he can only assign to the "efficient" will of God.

When he examines the link between the external world and the internal world-consciousness, Schleiermacher says it is "in the temporal frame and the spatial individualization of existence, upon which the beginnings of all sin depend."[102] Time and space *per se* are not sufficient causes of sin; they are only objectively necessary factors, upon which the vivification of subjective world-consciousness "depends." In order for sin actually to occur, there must be

---

[101]Ibid., #72,5.

[102]Ibid., #76,2.

a freely activated domination by the power of world-consciousness over the power of God-consciousness, but this empowerment of world-consciousness does occur in part due to its dependence on the objective presence of the physical world.

> Sin exists only where there is a powerlessness of the God-consciousness, and . . . develops in man in consequence of impressions received from the totality of finite existence.[103]

The multifarious feelings of world-consciousness are based upon its multifarious sources in the world, and the variety of these potential feelings seems determined at first to dominate the impressionable and inexperienced actual self-consciousness.[104] Schleiermacher thus acknowledges that even with the potentials being *formally* equal in the incipient stages of actual consciousness, the world-consciousness has the stronger *material* base, composed of finite impressions of the same ideal-real extraction as the finite self doing the actualization:

> Given an activity of the sensible self-consciousness to occupy a moment of time and to connect it with another: its exponent (*Exponent*) will be greater than that of the higher self-consciousness for uniting itself therewith; and given an activity of the higher self-consciousness, to occupy a moment of time through union with a determination of the sensible, its exponent will be less than that of the activity of the sensible for completing the moment for itself alone. Under these conditions no satisfaction of the impulse towards the God-consciousness will be possible.[105]

---

[103]Ibid., #65,1.

[104]Ibid., #8,2.

[105]Ibid., #11,2.

The "temporal frame and spatial individualization" of existence seems therefore to be what strengthens the "tendency" (*Richtung*) of the world-consciousness, to increase its "exponent" for achieving early actualization over the God-consciousness. It is the inherent inevitability of this tendency's realization, in contrast to the recessiveness of God-consciousness, which Schleiermacher identifies as the corruption, or subversion, in original sin:

> Original sin is called corruption of one's nature as contrasted with the original perfection, inasmuch as the latter in its true development has to some extent been subverted by original sin.[106]

The presence of the objective world becomes such an exponential force in eliciting the world-consciousness, in one respect, through the objective *knowledge* it presents, but in another respect because of the objective *socialization* which it also presents as a feature of the world. The social dimension of worldly incentives is brought in by Schleiermacher to emphasize how the plain physicality of the external world is amplified to the inner self by the social preoccupation with it. The corporate milieu of our experience of the external world involves all of us in the "weaknesses of . . . a narrow circle of descent and society,"[107] and this involvement in a particular social pattern of physicality is what he calls the corporate nature of original sin.[108]

Schleiermacher recognizes that our objective consciousness of the physical world is definitely facilitated by the social context, which enhances the importance of material things in objective consciousness, and thence to the subjective realm of world-consciousness. "The development of the sensuous life, that takes place

---

[106]Ibid., #71,2.

[107]Ibid., #94,3.

[108]Ibid., #71,3.

in all men before that of the spiritual, does not depend on the *individual alone*,"[109] and therefore "the sin of each, as regards its particular form, will be rooted in something beyond his own life."[110] The entrenched social involvement in the materiality of the world further enhances the sense of inevitability with which the sensible impulses impress themselves into our inward self-consciousness.

The phenomenological examination of how world-consciousness comes to dominate God-consciousness in the first stage of actualized existence thus reveals dual "incentives" from the objective world, which Schleiermacher identifies as spatio-temporal materiality and historical sociality. But in simply identifying these objective incentives to a subjective state, Schleiermacher always adds a further observation, suggesting the inevitability of the connection between the objective and subjective modes of consciousness. Such a sense of inevitability does come within the actualized phenomena of world-conscious domination, but Schleiermacher suggests that its source can only lie in the overpowered God-consciousness, as it reveals the overall determination of both its recessiveness and the dominance of the world-consciousness.

Having described in philosophical terms how the tendency toward original sin prevails over original perfection, Schleiermacher moves in his more theological references to describe how such a human eventuality issues from the overall pattern of divine determination. While disclaiming any effort to justify or to explain the divine will, Schleiermacher does claim to be able to describe the humanly experienced effects of that will, that is, the "efficient will" of God. It is in this sense of seeking an overall pattern in human experience that Schleiermacher must find a theological starting point in the state of redemption, to reflect upon the divine ordination effective in all stages of life:

---

[109]Ibid., #69,3 (emphasis mine).

[110]Ibid., #69,2.

> Although at the first creation of the human race only the imperfect state of human nature was manifested, yet eternally the appearance of the redeemer was already involved in that. So that, in whatever sense its fulfillment has to be conceived, the unity of the divine decree (*die Einheit des göttlichen Ratschlusses*) comes out with equal clearness whether we say that God ordained sin (*Gott habe ... die Sünde geordnet*) for man relatively to redemption, or that he put human nature under the law of earthly existence in the sense that, just as the sensuous self-consciousness developed first in each individual, while the God-consciousness came only later and up to a point gradually subjugated (*unterwirft*) the sensuous self-consciousness, so too the God-consciousness in the race to begin with was inadequate and impotent, and only later broke forth in perfection in Christ.[111]

Although Schleiermacher wishes to point out that in the absolute, commanding will of God, original perfection would prevail throughout every human life ("every moment of human activity might have been a product of the original perfection of man"[112]), he nevertheless finds phenomenological evidence that God "effectively" wills the interjection of original sin and actual sin. Although he always qualifies those statements that attribute sin to the ordination of God so that they include the context of human actualization, he still finds within the human phenomenon of sin such irrefragable inevitability that he can only "admit a universal imputation (*allgemeine Zurechnung*) of the first sin."[113]

We *know* of the imputation of sin, however, only as we come to know the imputation of grace in the state of redemption, and the inevitability of sin must therefore be described theologically only as that efficient means that has to obtain in order for redemption ultimately to obtain. "It is only from the absolute

---

[111] Ibid., #89,3.

[112] Ibid., #75,1.

[113] Ibid., #72,6.

sinlessness and the perfect spiritual power of the redeemer that we gain full knowledge of sin."[114]

The painful sense of tragic inevitability is changed in the redeemer into a joyful sense of consummated inevitability, for belief in him "is at once the basis of the full consciousness of sin as a derangement of our nature, and of faith in the possibility of redemption by the communication of the spiritual power so attested."[115] Christ finally demonstrates to us the real possibility of "original perfection," and by way of contrast, the awful actuality of that which we have followed out of "original sin."

THE PREDOMINANCE OF WORLD-CONSCIOUSNESS AS THE ACTUAL STATE OF SIN

The Reality of Sin as a State of Actual Self-Consciousness

Upon the occurrence of the first actually self-existent moment in life, persons find themselves to be irresitbly pulled into the ascendant pattern of dominance by world-consciousness and subservience by God-consciousness, and this pattern becomes the first actual state in the existential development of life. The incipient dominance of world-consciousness, which was original sin, now finds its full realization as it achieves the initial ascendancy in actual existence, and establishes the first real state of the self as that of actual sin.

The existence of sin as a feature of human life is known to be real precisely because it constitutes a fully actualized "state" of self-consciousness, that may be located in the developmental course of life as a "stage," with states lying before it and after it. The character of sin is not known by one within the state, however, just because it is a disjointed and expendable stage, which will be

---

[114]Ibid., #68,3.

[115]Ibid.

comprehended only when it has been disallowed and overcome by the state that follows.

That sin is a definite reality, in terms of human existence, is made clear when Schleiermacher refers to it as an actual state (*Zustand*) of feeling,[116] that is "that state of a hopeless incapacity in the spirit that prevails outside the sphere (*Gebiet*) of redemption."[117] Sin is a "fact ... as such"[118] because it is the state of distinct antithesis to that of redemption, "man's common state anterior to the entrance of redemption."[119]

Sin is therefore an actual state of the immediate self-consciousness, and is not to be equated with any sort of reflective or objective type of consciousness that might occur after the fact. Actual sin is not dependent upon a "consciousness *of* sin," even though Schleiermacher's terminology often obscures this point. What Schleiermacher means by "consciousness of sin" is a function of world-consciousness *within the later state of redemption*, but even there it still indicates a facet of immediate self-consciousness, which is unconfusedly sinful, and not an objectively conscious reflection about sin.

For those critics of Schleiermacher who would find his doctrine of sin to involve only a "subjectively projected sense of one's own failure," it is appropriate to point out here that the "subjectivity of sin" involves a fully actualized state of the subject's existence-relationships to God and to the world. As an actual state in the life of self-consciousness, "sin" connects both to the antecedent state of original sin and to the anticipated state of consciousness of sin in redemption. Yet, even as it relates to the before and to the after as an in-between "stage along life's

---

[116] Ibid., #63.

[117] Ibid., #66,2.

[118] Ibid., #80,1.

[119] Ibid., #64,2.

way," it distinctly establishes itself as a reality of life in the existential location in which it is found.

"Actual sin," or sin *per se*, is able to be described from a phenomenological standpoint only by one within the state, for its full derivation and outcome can be known only by the more comprehensive perspectives of philosophy and theology. Philosophy alone can comprehend the general *existenzial* structure of existence in which sin occurs, and theology alone can comprehend the specific *existenziell* process of which sin is but a fragmented part.

Neither can therefore present a complete picture of the place of sin in human existence, and it comes to Schleiermacher to develop a hybrid theoretical approach for such a task, an approach that he then calls the "philosophy of religion." It is the task of this hermeneutically hybrid theory to explain philosophically the workings of sin in self-consciousness, but from the perspective of the religious state of transformation of that sinful self-consciousness, a perspective that only theology can apply.

Schleiermacher tells us that from a purely philosophical point of view people *can* grasp that the state of sin is a confused and debilitating one, but that they can try to deal with their state only in further sinful pursuits of world-conscious gratification:

> The recognition of such a condition [of struggle, or opposition between two powers] undeniably finds a place in all religious communions. For the aim of all penances and purifications is to put an end to the consciousness of this condition or to the condition itself.[120]

The ultimate meaning of sin, however, can be grasped only from the later stage of redemption, in the reflection of theology, but at that stage the phenomenological insight that informed the sinful person *in situ* will no longer be available to provide a description of sin *per se*, that is, of sin without redemption.

---

[120]Ibid., #11,3.

A description of the sense of sin as the exclusive content even of merely detached portions of life . . . could find no verification in the Christian consciousness itself; such a description would therefore be no doctrine of faith.[121]

The reality of sin may thus be ascertained at best under the uncertain conditions of a humanly developed philosophy of religion, in which humans try to comprehend the contingencies of their finite existence as somehow lying under an infinite power which both controls and transforms that existence. It is with such a tenuous but inescapable religio-philosophical perspective that we now attempt to understand with Schleiermacher what is entailed in the actual state of sin.

The Dominance of World-Consciousness as Actual Sin

The term "actual sin" (*wirkliche Sünde*) is used by Schleiermacher with a caveat[122] that his usage is decidedly different from the usage in classical theology, although it is still to be seen as a basic counterpoint to "original sin" (*Erbsünde*). Traditional theologians, according to Schleiermacher, had interpreted original sin as a corporeally and historically inherited state of nature, and thus had seen actual sins as present manifestations of the received sinfulness.

Schleiermacher wishes to reassess the sense of "originality" so that it no longer refers to a phylogenetic nature, historically transmitted to the race from an original sinner, but rather to an ontogenetic state at the foundation of each individual's life. In keeping with this view, Schleiermacher comes to see actual sin as the state of actualization of each individual's own original tendency to sin, which actualizes what before was simply a preliminary stage of the same individual's life.

The key to Schleiermacher's understanding of sin is his ontological framework for viewing the process of existence, in which the original stage of

---

[121]Ibid., #64,1.

[122]Ibid., #69, postscript.

balance between the potencies gives way to the first stage of full actualization of one potency as dominant over the other. The actualization in self-consciousness can be regarded, as has been noted, both in particular moments and in continuing states of similar moments, and it is to such an ontologically conceived state that the actuality of sin refers.

In keeping with his existential-ontological categorization of the flowing of moments into states, Schleiermacher comes to view "actual sin" as both the momentary acts (*Taten*) of sin and the general state of actualizing sinfulness (*Sündhaftigkeit*) into which these acts arrange themselves.[123] The sheer accumulation of particular sins makes the state of sin more and more ingrained, but on the other hand, the universal inevitability of original sin, which led into actual sinfulness, means that no particular act within the state of sinfulness can be a worse "sin" than any other:

> All actual sins must rank as equal not only in respect of their nature and character but also of their origin; for every such sin is a manifestation of the universal sinfulness, and represents a victory [in actual self-consciousness], though but momentary or partial, of flesh over spirit.[124]

The universally inevitable quality of original sin so qualifies the succeeding state of actual sin that every moment within the state manifests the same type of sinful actualization of world-consciousness over God-consciousness.

> The disposition of sin, of which our apprehension is at once inward and timeless, would not be an actuality unless it were constantly manifesting itself.
>
> So original sin necessarily has a part in every inner act of every man in whom it is present. Throughout the entire range of sinful

---

[123] Ibid., #81,2.

[124] Ibid., #74,1.

humanity there is not a single perfectly good action, i.e. one that purely expresses the potency of the God-consciousness; nor is there one perfectly pure moment, i.e. one in which something does not exist in secret antagonism to the God-consciousness.[125]

The character of the state of sin is defined by Schleiermacher basically in terms of the continuing dominance of world-consciousness over God-consciousness in the moments of actual self-consciousness. But Schleiermacher does occasionally rely on simpler alternative terms which he also feels may adequately characterize the nature of the state of sinfulness. One such metaphorical image of sin is the term "bondage" (*Gebundenheit*), by which Schleiermacher indicates the state of incapacity of the God-consciousness caused by the dominance of world-consciousness.

(Sin) is the absence of facility for introducing the God-consciousness into the course of our actual lives, and retaining it there. . . . Under these conditions no satisfaction of the impulse towards the God-consciousness will be possible; and so, if such a satisfaction is to be attained, a redemption is necessary, since this state is nothing but a kind of *bondage* of the feeling of absolute dependence.[126]

The "state of bondage" is logically the forerunner of the "state of redemption," in which the "incapacitated" God-consciousness is to be empowered and set free. But before redemption, human beings are only vaguely aware of their lost and struggling state of sin, that "state of a hopeless incapacity of the spirit that prevails outside the sphere of redemption."[127]

The diminished capacity of the God-consciousness, or "spirit," suggests another of Schleiermacher's biblically based metaphors for sin, which is the state

---

[125]Ibid., #73,1.

[126]Ibid., #11,2.

[127]Ibid., #66,2.

of the "flesh." Although Schleiermacher recognizes that "flesh" can in one sense refer to the normal potency of the world-consciousness, he further recognizes that even in the state of original sin "flesh" connotes the tendency toward *dominance* by the world-consciousness. When original sin has thus been capacitated in the state of actual sin, Schleiermacher says that in every sense this is *the* state of the flesh.

> What gives a moment the character of sin is the self-centered activity of the flesh, for all activities of the flesh are good when subservient to the spirit, and all are evil when severed from it.[128]

What characterizes the state of sin is not the mere presence of the fleshly power, which is naturally given in the ontological structure of any state, but rather the dominant assertiveness of the power, the "antagonism of the flesh."[129] Combining his metaphors, Schleiermacher calls sin "a bondage of the determinative power of the spirit, due to the independence of the sensuous functions [flesh]."[130]

Because in the state of sin "the sensuous consciousness alone is determinative"[131] the pleasure-pain vector will naturally orient itself so as to align pleasure with the satisfied world-consciousness and pain with the dispossessed God-consciousness. In the state of sin, says Schleiermacher, "the sensuous self-consciousness by reason of its having been gratified is affected with pleasure, but the higher, owing to the impotence of the God-consciousness, with pain."[132] So strong is the tone of satisfaction with the dominant world awareness—of both the

---

[128] Ibid., #74,1.

[129] Ibid., #71,4; #71,3.

[130] Ibid., #66,2.

[131] Ibid., #107,1.

[132] Ibid., #66,1.

natural world and the human world—that Schleiermacher also recognizes the contribution of social acclimation to sensual enhancement, and calls it the "state of fellowship of sinfulness" among the human race.[133]

The question of how genuinely humane can be the sense of fellowship among sinful persons is another issue, however, and raises the further question of whether sin for Schleiermacher is more an ethical or a religious category. The question on Schleiermacher's terms would be whether the assertiveness of world-consciousness (and its preoccupation with the self's sensuous satisfaction) is a more crucial problem (ethical) than the incapacitation of the God-consciousness (religious). Like most religious philosophers, however, Schleiermacher tries to bridge the perspectival gap in order to point out that sin in reality functions in both senses, as a state that actualizes both a consciousness of the world and a consciousness of God.

> Actual sin may be either more an expression of appetite, or more a positive obscuration, i.e., a vitiation of the God-consciousness. We cannot wholly separate the two, for the one ever evokes the other.[134]

The key to Schleiermacher's view again is the polar-dialectical reciprocity in actual self-consciousness, in which neither potency of self-consciousness is able to occur without the composite presence of the other. Sin is *at the same time* the relative "being" of the sensuous consciousness (ethical sin) and the relative "non-being" of the God-consciousness (religious sin), since in every state of actualization only one can be the dominant factor, although both are present. The power of world-consciousness, which is the sensuous "expression of appetite," must in its process of dominating actual self-consciousness obscure, or "vitiate," the power of God-consciousness.

---

[133]Ibid., #91,2.

[134]Ibid., #74,2.

In regard specifically to the world, which the sin-prone world-consciousness both uses and abuses, it certainly would be said that the state of sin has all-pervasive ethical consequences. The sinful state of world-dominance relates itself to the world as "a self-enclosed life of feeling within a sensuous vital unity, to which all sympathetic feeling for others and for the whole is subordinated."[135] The malproportioned dominance of world-consciousness in actual self-consciousness involves a malproportionment *within* world-consciousness itself, so that the self's relation to the world is more self-oriented than mutually reciprocal with the world.

The world-consciousness in its state of sinful dominance becomes so "self-enclosed" that its proper feeling of relative dependence upon the world becomes too dependent upon the natural world, and not dependent enough upon the human world. Thus the polar reciprocity of active dependence and receptive dependence upon the world is dichotomized: the sinful self feels only *receptivity* toward the world of nature, with no reciprocal willingness to exercise active control over it, while it feels only controlling *activity* toward the world of humanity, without willingness to be receptive or "sympathetic" toward others.

In both cases, the world-consciousness is asserting its misconstrued domination of actual self-consciousness in ways that further misconstrue its own relations, or dependencies, upon the world. The ethical ramifications occur within the sphere of the self's relationships to the world, both to nature and to humans, but these misconstructed dependencies *within* world-consciousness must finally be seen as manifestations of the overall misconstruction of self-consciousness *per se*, in which world-consciousness has thwarted the proper role of God-consciousness. It is, in Schleiermacher's view, the fundamental misassertion by world-consciousness of dominance over God-consciousness, or the religious aspect of sin, which devolves into the subsidiary misconstructions within world-consciousness, or the ethical aspect of sin.

---

[135]Ibid., #101,2.

Because it is the God-consciousness that properly should dominate in actual self-consciousness, the situation of its bondage is naturally the central issue in the state of sin, and this means that sin is basically a problem of a religious type. That sin is a religious issue is only understood from the later stage of redemption, however, for the actual state of sin can allow one to understand one's difficulties only ethically, that is, as misapprehensions *within* the relations of world-consciousness *per se*. Sin becomes a religious type of category because its larger significance is that it is a state of blockage of the God-consciousness, and anything that involves the God-consciousness must be considered religious (*religiös*).

Sin is not a pious (*fromm*) category, however, for a pious attribution can be made only in reference to the final state of piety, or redeemed God-consciousness. For this reason sin cannot be a proper category of consideration by theology, since theology is able to reflect directly only upon states and attributes of piety. That sin is generally religious, rather than specifically pious, in its reference, means that Schleiermacher must regard the "state of sin" as a general category of existence to be considered by philosophy of religion.[136] Philosophy of religion, as noted earlier, would stand somewhere between ethical philosophy, which deals with mankind's relations to the world, and theology, which deals with mankind's relations to God. As a state of human existence, and as a category of religious analysis, sin will therefore involve purely ethical considerations, but may only intimate at purely pious considerations.

The Suppression of God-consciousness in Sin as the Incipient Impartation of Grace

If the actual state of sin is to be categorized more from the *ethical*-philosophical side in its ramifications in world-consciousness, it is then to be categorized more from the *religious*-philosophical side in its ramifications in God-consciousness. It is now our task to examine precisely what happens to the

---

[136]Ibid., #2,2 and #2,3.

God-consciousness as it is pressed into subservience in the actual moments and the actual state of sin.

Schleiermacher insists above all that the God-consciousness continues to exist as a fully viable potency and element of actual self-consciousness even throughout the moments of its subjugation in the state of sin. The promise of its original perfection and the intimations of its ultimate redemption provide it with a viability that it does not comprehend in the moments of sin, but that will be religiously interpreted from the perspective of its entire development.

The impulses of God-consciousness under sin reveal, first of all, the "ineradicable residuum of the original impartation of the divine,"[137] which somehow is now confused as to its source and identity. Looking forward, however, even "in the sins of the natural man . . . there is always the now deeper and now fainter shadow of the good, namely an acquiescent presentiment or imagining of a state free from inward conflict."[138] In the condition of sinfulness, therefore, "a consciousness of God was never determinative of [the actual moment], being but casual and fleeting; the sensuous consciousness alone was determinative."[139]

In Schleiermacher's version of the *imago dei*, the "residuum (*Rest*) of the divine," it is clear that he wants to present the God-consciousness as a distinctive, perduring ontological element of existence which is somehow disposed into a condition of inappropriate actualization. What then is the nature of the God-consciousness as subjected to the confusion and cross-purposes of an actualizing self-consciousness under the control of world-consciousness? Schleiermacher's basic phenomenological description of God-consciousness here is that it exemplifies the pain aspect of the antithesis of pleasure and pain, which

---

[137]Ibid., #108,6.

[138]Ibid., #74,4.

[139]Ibid., #107,1.

THE STAGES OF DEVELOPMENT IN ACTUAL SELF-CONSCIOUSNESS 157

in every conscious moment characterizes the two potencies, according to whichever is more prominent and whichever is more recessive.

In the state of sin, therefore, "the sensuous self-consciousness by reason of its having been gratified is affected with pleasure, but the higher, owing to the impotence of God-consciousness, with pain."[140] The God-consciousness still *seeks*, because of its nature, its rightful place as "the determining power," but because it comes "to feel limited, pain is bound up with it."[141] We do not at once perceive the full implications of the state, but later we will understand that sin is its character "whenever the God-consciousness which is put with an inner state . . . determines our self-consciousness as pain."[142]

The sense of pain in the God-consciousness thus occurs as the vectoral opposite of the sense of pleasure in the world-consciousness, as together they constitute a characteristic moment of the sinful state. The feeling of pain in the suppressed God-consciousness is also referred to by Schleiermacher as the feeling of "guilt," for this conveys the sense that the world-consciousness is responsible for inhibiting the power of the God-consciousness. The guilt, or displeasure, of the God-consciousness is the reciprocal opposite of the concurrent pleasure, or satisfaction, which reigns in the world-consciousness during sin.

The guilt, or pain, of the God-consciousness is shown in its induced, vectored relationship with the satisfaction, or pleasure, of world-consciousness in diagram 1. (See next page.)

---

[140]Ibid., #66,1.

[141]Ibid., #62,1.

[142]Ibid., #66, int.

DIAGRAM 1: CHARACTERISTICS OF SIN AND EVIL

```
                          The Passing Moments of Sin
                          into Moments of Evil
  The      WORLD
           CONSCIOUSNESS    SIN  → evokes  → EVIL
  State                    Satisfaction ─evokes→ Hindrance
                           (pleasure)            (pain)
  of
                ↓
  Sin      dominates        ↓                    ↓
                           induces              induces
  (and            ↓
                            ↓                    ↓
  Evil)    GOD-            Guilt               Punishment
           CONSCIOUSNESS   (pain)              (pleasure)
                           ******─evokes→******
                           Holiness            Justice
                           of God              Of God
```

Because world-consciousness is predominant, it is inevitable that its pleasure must antithetically redound to, or induce, the pain of God-consciousness.

A related type of moment that occurs within the state of sin is also shown in the diagram, that is, the occurrence of evil as a sub-type of dominant worldly feeling, evoked by the pleasure of sin. Whereas most world-conscious moments in the state of sin interact with the world in a self-satisfactory way, some moments in the state that actualizes the dominant world-consciousness will find the interaction with the world to be painful, or an "evil" hindrance to the senses. But, says Schleiermacher, sin is the primary feeling, and evil is a subsidiary type of feeling evoked by sin itself:

THE STAGES OF DEVELOPMENT IN ACTUAL SELF-CONSCIOUSNESS 159

>Man, were he without sin [sensual satisfaction], would not feel what are merely hindrances of sensuous functions as evils; the very fact that he does so feel them is due to sin, and hence that type of evil, subjectively considered, is a penalty of sin.[143]

The feeling of evil is simply the feeling of sin exposing itself to the world to the point of saturation, to the point that the world-consciousness becomes overloaded by the world, whether natural or human, and finds in it hindrances rather than satisfactions. Certainly, says Schleiermacher, the immensely varied nature of worldly sensations coming into the completely open world-consciousness is bound on occasion to displease it, and when this occurs it senses pain, and projects "evil" (*Übel*) upon the world. "Evil arises only with sin, but given sin, it arises inevitably."[144]

When "the evil moments come" to a sinful person, and the person "no longer takes pleasure" in the dominant potency of the *world-consciousness*, but finds it instead a source of pain, in those evil moments the *God-consciousness* is reciprocally present in its own way—which is with the antithetical feeling of pleasure, in that the dominant world-consciousness is being punished for its sinful excesses. The sensible hindrances (*Hemmungen*),[145] which the world naturally presents at times to the world-consciousness, reciprocally induce in the God-consciousness a sense of just punishment, a sense that evil is "the penalty of sin."

When the God-consciousness in moments of evil is moved with a sense of pleasure, induced as opposite to the pain in world-consciousness, it is also aware that it stands in a line of sequential evocation by the previous sinful moments of God-consciousness, in which the God-consciousness was moved to pain. Considering just the sequential progression of impulses in God-consciousness

---

[143] Ibid., #76,2.

[144] Ibid., #75,1.

[145] Ibid., #84,2.

itself, we find that the passage from moments of sin to moments of evil evokes a passage from a pained, or guilty, God-consciousness to a pleasureable, or punished God-consciousness. The God-consciousness still is suppressed in both these moments by world-consciousness, but it finds the suppression to be variously painful or pleasureable, depending upon the type of moment of the world domination.

The human feelings of guilt and punishment in the state of sin are thus basically similar in that they are responses of God-consciousness to the improper domination of world-consciousness, that is, they are the conscious human expressions of God's own disposition toward our worldly assertions of sin and evil. The sense of guilt that humans have is thus their reflection of the divine determination of holiness toward sin, and their sense of penal desert is their reflection of the divine determination of justice toward evil.

> Only one relationship to the divine holiness (*Heiligkeit*) and justice (*Gerechtigkeit*) is proper to the corporate life of sinfulness, namely the self-consciousness of guilt (*Schuld*) and merited punishment (*Strafwürdigkeit*).[146]

Just as in every other "feeling of absolute dependence," the feelings of the God-consciousness here are seen by Schleiermacher to be self-conscious representations of God's external and absolute determination of the self. The resultant feelings of God that we have simply manifest the divine causality that occasions them, even in our state of sinful obstruction of those feelings.

> By the holiness of God we understand that divine causality through which in all human life conscience [guilt] is found conjoined with the need of redemption.[147]

---

[146]Ibid., #107,1.

[147]Ibid., #83, int.

Schleiermacher then continues:

> The justice of God is that divine causality through which in the state of universal sinfulness there is ordained a connection between sin and evil.[148]

In the last analysis it is the absolute causality of God which is seen to have ordained the connection between sin and evil in the world-consciousness, and therefore the connection between guilt and punishment which is induced in the God-consciousness.

> In our consciousness the connection between sin and evil is actually and even universally made—this is really the consciousness of penal desert, which in the human mind is as truly the creation of the divine justice as [guilt] is the creation of divine holiness.[149]

As he says of sin, Schleiermacher aims to say also of evil, that it is not simply an imagined veil over consciousness, but is rather a definite reality of the actualizing-self-consciousness type of existence. Further, evil is seen to be just as real as the sin that evokes it, because it, too, lies under the efficient ordination of God as a state of human reality ingredient to the process of redemption. The specific purpose of evil and its associated sense of punishment is to prevent humankind from falling utterly into the "unchecked habit"[150] of sin.

> Just as the consciousness of sin as necessarily entailing penalty [as evil]—a consciousness due to the divine justice—is possible only on the assumption that guilt is due to the divine holiness, so without that consciousness of penal liability, guilt would have no means of gaining a

---

[148] Ibid., #84, int.

[149] Ibid., #84,2.

[150] Ibid., #84,3.

secure hold in any human soul still under the dominion of the flesh, and thus no means of generating there a consciousness of the need of redemption.[151]

Guilt and punishment may be reckoned as prompted, or "induced," by the world-feelings of sin and evil, but because they are feelings of God-determination they must also be recognized as "superinduced" by divine impartation. The feelings are "generated" in us as a means of instigating the God-consciousness to be open to redemption. Our guilt, or displeasure, with the bad "is wrought in us by the divine causality" just to generate "our own displeasure with the fact that the effective power of the God-consciousness falls short of the clearness of our apprehension."[152] Just as sin and evil are seen to be ordained only as implemental stages in the accomplishment of redemption, so also we must see "the consciousness of guilt and penal desert being ordained for men by God only in relation to redemption."[153]

That God does not command *specific* evils as punishments for specific sins of individuals is a further corollary of Schleiermacher's "universalized" view of the absolute determination of God. Evil as flowing from sin seems rather to be the universal "efficient" will of God, which applies corporately to the whole human race *qua* corporately ordained toward redemption. Whatever particular sensuous hindrances that occur as evils in individual lives thus are not to be seen as *quid pro quo* penalties exacted for sins, but rather as general indicators that the state of sinful worldliness should give way to a state where pain in the world-consciousness would not have to be felt as evil.

The suffering that occurs in evil is not seen by Schleiermacher as a penalty in the orthodox retributive view of the just God dealing ethically with unjust

---

[151]Ibid., #84,4.

[152]Ibid., #83,3.

[153]Ibid., #109,3.

humankind. (Nor certainly would it be seen in accordance with the tragic view of evil, in which suffering is mysteriously imposed by an arbitrary God upon unsuspecting humans.) Schleiermacher rather tries to emphasize the universal instrumentality of evil as leading human beings into a deeper awareness of the universal good for which they are destined. This view of evil therefore tries to steer a middle course, by maintaining that humans *are* sinful, but in need of correction and not retribution, while also maintaining that the nature of evil *is* mysterious, but ultimately to be comprehended in the universal ordination of God.

Schleiermacher clearly maintains this instrumental view of evil when he acknowledges that sin and evil *are* realities experienced in the individual's life, but that they are not ultimately real in the same sense as the universal reality of mankind's determination to good.

> That even the most serious [evils], considered purely by themselves . . . are not punishments, but incentives rather to the development of the spirit, is taught by Christ himself with reference to the man born blind.[154]

This comprehension of the true nature of evil is not, of course, evident to persons who are suffering, because their state of sinful preoccupation with world-consciousness, both pleasureful and painful, prevents their seeing the true meaning of God-consciousness.[155] Sinful persons can comprehend only the fearful sense of being punished in their God-consciousness, without understanding the ultimate goal of the divine justice.

> In virtue of their capacity for the God-consciousness all men certainly are also objects of the divine love; but the divine love does not realize itself in them simply as such; rather, starting from the fear of God (which was, of course, the prevailing religious temper under the law) they at most get

---

[154]Ibid., #76,2.

[155]Ibid., #5,4.

> through to the negative consciousness that the supreme being is devoid of jealousy—which is still very far from being a recognition of the divine love. That only comes with the efficacious working of redemption, and it comes from Christ.[156]

The feeling of punishment in evil, or the fear of God, is thus the beginning of human wisdom, at least to the point of accepting that the punishment derives from a transcendent justice, even if its working remains mysterious. The God-consciousness will later be seen to have used both the sense of guilt and the sense of punishment to stimulate at least some kind of awareness by the person of a transcendent power at work in the persons's life, although under the dominance of sin these divine impartations could only be called prevenient grace.

> In the common life of sinfulness, we find many sorts of regret [guilt] . . . which show genuine pain at the general human state of sinfulness as illustrated in one's own person, but they do not develop into a continuous inward movement or state amounting to the dawn of living faith.
> Such stimulations . . . are to be regarded as divinely caused, and indeed involved in the divine ordinance which places all men in relation to the redeemer . . . and are ascribed to the prevenient grace of God.[157]

Such stimulations, or stirrings, of the suppressed God-consciousness cannot be recognized by sinful people for what they are, but because God's commanding power, even in that instrumental stage of sin, is aimed toward redemption, we will from the long-range point of view see all such stimulations of God-consciousness as instances of "preparatory grace." The sinful-evil ascendancy of *world*-consciousness is thus not regarded as being in the commanded will of God in the way that the opposing struggle of the suppressed *God*-consciousness is.

---

[156]Ibid., #166,2.

[157]Ibid., #108,2.

In virtue of the teleological character of Christian piety, both the imperfect stage of the higher life [sin], as also the challenge to it [guilt], appear in our self-consciousness as facts due to our own individual action—though we do not feel responsible for the latter [guilt] in the same way as the former. In virtue, however, of the peculiar character of Christianity this challenge is also apprehended in our self-consciousness as the act of the redeemer. These two points of view can be reconciled only by supposing that this challenge is the act of the redeemer become our own act.[158]

The "challenge" to sinful world-consciousness presented by God-consciousness as the feeling of guilt is from the subsequent standpoint of redemption clearly acknowledged to have been the work of the redeemer, inspiring and activating the God-consciousness. Even though the feeling of guilt occurs as our own act, it is nonetheless regarded by Schleiermacher as originated by a source beyond our instantiation of it. This tentative revival of our blocked feeling of God can be understood only after its full efficacy is achieved, but it will then be known to have been efficacious in overcoming sin only because it was a direct impartation of divine power through the office of the redeemer.

Humans, to be sure, do not in sin follow what is being done to prepare their God-consciousness for re-empowerment, but through the dawning acuteness of their guilt and punishment they begin to demonstrate an "acquiescent presentiment"[159] which is at least a receptivity to grace.[160] Such a presentiment will grow into a thirst, or desire, for redemption immediately before the advent of grace, and the person will then recognize it as the person's only participation in the process of restoring God-consciousness to its rightful position in life.

---

[158]Ibid., #100,1.

[159]Ibid., #74,4.

[160]Ibid., #94,3.

> In the matter [of redemption] we posit, on the one side, an initial divine activity which is supernatural, but at the same time a vital human receptivity in virtue of which alone that supernatural can become a natural fact of history.[161]

The receptivity, however, is only the human side of the self-consciousness of absolute determination, and so must ultimately admit that its preparation for grace was absolutely determined in the same way as was its acceptance of grace.[162]

Even though the God-consciousness while in the state of sin is definitely obscured and suppressed, it is still the working power of the absolute determinant which has effected its own submission under the terms of conscious existence, and which will ultimately effect its release as well. Just as much as God will be recognized as having ordained sin, so also will God be recognized to have ordained the respondent guilt, which involved the incipient presence of grace. "We can now see the appropriateness of linking the first consciousness of sin [guilt], due to the accession of the God-consciousness, with the first presentiment of redemption."[163]

Even in its submissive existential state, the God-consciousness will be seen to have been determined into its situation by its source, and then to have been determined into its recipient reassertion through the same preparatory power of grace. In regard to the apparent antinomy of freedom and determination, here again Schleiermacher clearly falls onto the side of divine determination. *Sola gratia*, rather than *sola fide*, is his watchword, for the conduct of the God-consciousness, even under its subjugation by world-consciousness, can only reveal that the absolute power of God is fully at work within the seemingly intransigent condition of human sin.

---

[161]Ibid., #88,4.

[162]Ibid., #108,6.

[163]Ibid., #71,3.

As regards the divine attributes, it is of course evident that statements concerning God cannot issue from a condition of alienation from God, but are only possible when a man is in some sense turned again toward him. But not even when sin is viewed from the standpoint of a paramount God-consciousness can we conceive of divine attributes that have to do with sin apart from its disappearance as a result of redemption.[164]

THE PREDOMINANCE OF GOD-CONSCIOUSNESS AS THE ACTUAL STATE OF GRACE

The Reality of Grace as a State of Actual Self-Consciousness

The actual state of grace is the temporally final "state" of actual self-consciousness to be reached in the process of life, and it is also the qualitatively ultimate "state" which may be attained in the dialectical reciprocity of dominant potencies which animates existence. From the standpoint of the earlier states, what happens in the state of grace might be only another quantitative state in an indefinite line of temporal succession, doomed to a continually misproportioned alternation of dominance. From the standpoint of the state of grace itself, however, it is secured in the revelation that it is indeed the final possible state in the temporal process, because it is the qualitatively ultimate stage of existential proportion, which the potencies before had only been struggling to achieve.

Schleiermacher wants to maintain two emphases in his doctrine of the state of grace: first, that it is still an actual state of the self-consciousness, within the ontologically comprehensible development of human existence, and second, that it is somehow also a transcendentally inspired state, to be fully comprehended only as a stage uniquely beyond the stages that preceded it. This view of grace is therefore an example of Schleiermacher's fundamental doctrine that the "natural"

---

[164]Ibid., #64,2.

realm is always open to, even if essentially determined by, the "supernatural" realm.

In one sense, Schleiermacher wants to maintain that grace obtains as a state within the ontological framework of the human being's "natural" development, that it is a state of existent actuality, even if it is transcendentally originated. In this regard, Schleiermacher emphasizes the continuity of the stages of existence, believing that every stage, even from the original stage of pre-actuality, is ordained in a definite way by the absolute source and origin:

> Although at the first creation of the human race only the imperfect state of human nature was manifested, yet eternally the appearance of the redeemer was already involved in that. So that, in whatever sense its fulfillment has to be conceived, the unity of the divine decree comes out with equal clearness.[165]

This continuity between creation and redemption is analogous to that between nature and supernature, for both antitheses suggest the absolute unity underlying even the very first and the very last of human life. This continuity must also include the middle stage, the stage of sin, as being ordained by God in a particular sense "relative to redemption," for "everything that belongs to the [sinful] period of the world must have a share in the relation to the redeemer."[166]

Schleiermacher's doctrine of the ontological continuity of life thus emphasizes the insight that redemption can actually occur only because it is the state that fulfills creation and supercedes the sin that has abridged creation. In spite of this sequential relationship *within* the temporal succession of existence, however, Schleiermacher maintains as the other aspect of the doctrine of grace that it occurs with the ultimacy and finality that it does because it is an

---

[165]Ibid., #89,3.

[166]Ibid.

exceptional infusion from *beyond* the natural course of existence. The "general revelation" in God-consciousness throughout all previous existence is now superceded, even if fulfilled, by the "special revelation" of redemption.

> To the power of the God-consciousness in our souls, just because we are conscious of it as not due to our own agency, we give the name "grace," and (abstracting from the universal divine cooperation without which sin itself were impossible) ascribe to it a special divine impartation.[167]

Even though God's ordination of our entire existential process is universally cooperative (in the "efficient will") in all the developmental stages of life, God's ordination of the singularly "commanded" stage of redemption is carried out with a "special divine impartation" (*besondern göttlichen Mitteilung*).[168] It is in this mysterious sense of a special dispensation, even within the universal determination of God over all human life, that we must view redemption, and try to understand its status as a uniquely consummated stage in life, in radical contrast to the former stage of sin which preceded it.

> The gracious forgiveness of sins is not an individual decree or act bearing on the single life, nor is it merely declaratory; it is one that emancipates from the sphere of guilt and penal desert, and one that is general—being fulfilled, indeed, at some point of time for each individual, but being then really fulfilled, and needing no repetition.[169]

If the state of grace is that which is utterly special and fulfilled, in a way that the former stages of life were not, what then still remains to characterize it as a stage of the same conscious life, to enable humans to know that they still are

---

[167] Ibid., #80,1.

[168] Ibid.

[169] Ibid., #111,3.

finite creatures, bounded by the same actually self-conscious existence? According to Schleiermacher, what remains of the old creation, even under the terms of the new, is the same tendency of world-consciousness to desire moments of dominance over the now empowered God-consciousness, and this vestigial remain of the sinful past is what will always connect humans with their individual existential history. It is a part of the universal divine ordination, says Schleiermacher, that even with the special impartation of power in redemption, "with the acceptance of such a redemption there is always conjoined a backward look to sin as prior to it."[170]

Just as the world-consciousness is ontologically conjoined in every moment with the God-consciousness, so also the sinful propensity is existentially joined *in every moment of existence* to the propensity for Godliness, even in the redeemed state where the Godly propensity has achieved dominance. "While [sin and grace] are antithetic, they are only such as in the religious life of the Christian are conjoined in every moment, though always in varied measure."[171] Even the redeemed Christians find that their sinful history of world-conscious predominance will never be totally erased from their existential propensities, and so "every Christian is conscious both of sin and of grace as always combined with each other and never dissociated."[172]

Indeed, the bi-polar antithesis of elements in every moment and state of life means that neither element can really find meaning except as in comparative conjunction with the other. It is for this reason that grace could never exemplify its profound meaning did it not exist in comparative juxtaposition to, and by being always conjoined with, the continued impulse for sin.

"As we never have a consciousness of grace without a consciousness of sin, we must also assert that the existence of sin alongside grace is ordained for

---

[170]Ibid., #63,2.

[171]Ibid., #63,3.

[172]Ibid., #64,1.

us by God."[173] Even in light of the sense of a special divine ordination in the triumph of redemption over sin, our experience makes us believe that the divine ordination also "entails that sin even in the process of disappearing should continue to exist side by side with grace."[174]

That "sin" still exists alongside grace is a further indication of the overall mystery of the divine ordination, but Schleiermacher says that we must accept it as so because we do indeed find remains of sin in the phenomena of our redeemed self-consciousness. The distinction between moments and states of actual self-consciousness is crucial here, for Schleiermacher believes that once the state of grace has entered, the *state* of sin is forever past, and that only random *moments* of sin may still occur.

Such moments, however, can never again fall into sufficient quantitative succession to comprise a qualitative state of sin, and the redeemed person may always be assured that the occasional moments of sin have no more power for lasting dominance within that person's life. Because particular moments of sinful worldliness are ever possible, however, the basically graceful moments in this state still will contain the world-consciousness as a potential whose past and present evinces the propensity for sinful dominance.

The state of grace is seen by Schleiermacher to be an actual state of self-consciousness, typical as well as unique, in the further regard that to it is attached the antithesis of pleasure and pain, which is the emotional vector of the dominance-submission antithesis. In this state, the God-consciousness is the basically dominant potency, which thus evinces a feeling of pleasure, or joy, and the world-consciousness is the submissive potency, which evinces a feeling of pain, or sorrow.

---

[173]Ibid., #80, int.

[174]Ibid., #80,2.

> But now in this [state of grace] as in other states of experience (as there is no such state as absolute joy . . . of the God-consciousness) pleasure and pain are by no means to be regarded as so separate from each other that one of them might in some circumstances actually exist without the other.[175]

The presence of the impulse toward sinful domination is still evident even in the suppressed world-consciousness, and it is therefore ever the source of residual sorrow even to the basically joyful God-consciousness. Even in the state of redemption, says Schleiermacher,

> The actual individual self-consciousness bears witness to [sin] in many a moment of sorrow [of world-consciousness], where the sorrow is assuaged by the simultaneous presence of the constant factor [joy of the God-consciousness]. At other moments, the self-consciousness is a joy that passes into humility because its only right to exist is found in what assuages the sorrow lying so near it.[176]

The joy of the God-consciousness obtains because of its definitive triumph over world-consciousness, and because of the self's newly found "ease in evoking pious feeling, which goes along with religious pleasure."[177] We are ever humbled, however, because of the residual reminders of the impulses to sin, and our awareness that "the facility with which we are able to graft the God-consciousness on the various sensuous excitations" is the imparted power of grace ascommunicated by the redeemer.[178] It is thus the external power of God which truly underlies the joy of our internal God-consciousness, and which makes us truly sorry for the sinful tendency of world-consciousness.

---

[175]Ibid., #62,1.

[176]Ibid., #110,3.

[177]Ibid., #32,1.

[178]Ibid., #63,2.

We are conscious of all approximations to the state of blessedness which occur in the Christian life as being grounded in a new divinely-effected corporate life, which works in opposition to the corporate life of sin and the misery which develops in it ... for approximation to the condition of blessedness [in God-consciousness] is the real opposite of the misery [of world-consciousness].[179]

The Reality of Grace as Communicated by the Redeemer

The basic reason that Schleiermacher believes the state of grace to be singularly transported beyond the other states of existence is that the Christian finds it to be empowered by the utterly singular existence of Christ, the redeemer. It is the actualized power of Christ to have had a perfectly dominant God-consciousness and a perfectly submissive world-consciousness, which is ordained by God now to be communicated to us. It is this power which effects in us the previously unimaginable change from our pattern of sin-dominance to our pattern of grace-dominance.

The process of communication of this power in transforming the dominance-submission pattern of human life is what Schleiermacher calls the process of redemption, and through it we pass from the state of sin into the state of grace. Redemption for Schleiermacher is both the moment of passage between the states, and the continuing process of growing confirmation of the new state of grace.

The moment of transformation, or regeneration, is that in which the God-consciousness is empowered by the redeemer into its first living moment of actual domination; the process of confirmation, or sanctification, is that in which the God-consciousness is empowered to establish a continuous state of dominant moments, ever more secure against the occasional incursions of sin.[180]

---

[179]Ibid., #87, int. and #87,1.

[180]Ibid., #106.

The *moment* of regeneration is thus seen by Schleiermacher to be so eventful because it signals the first instance of the entire *state* of being sanctified, and both the moment and the state to which it will belong are termed by Schleiermacher as "redemption," or as "grace." The fundamental point, however, is that the moment signifies such a singular state because it is more than just a typical moment of human self-consciousness—it is a moment of unique divine self-impartation through the medium of the redeemer.

The divine impartation of grace becomes the human event of grace because the redeemer is ordained to bridge the gap between the supernatural and the natural realms:

> We posit, on the one side, an initial divine activity which is supernatural, but at the same time a vital human receptivity in virtue of which alone the supernatural can become a natural fact of history.
>
> So, too, in relation to the redeemer himself, the new corporate life is no miracle, but simply the supernatural becoming natural.[181]

Here again Schleiermacher falls back upon his fundamental explanatory theory of absolute divine determination to explain just *how* it is that a "natural" human state can be transformed by a putatively separate "supernatural" power. The mediating being of Christ seems to exemplify the divine determination to bridge and even to combine the implicit differences between divine and humane.

> The influence of Christ, therefore, consists solely in the human communication of the word, in so far as that communication embodies Christ's word and continues the indwelling divine power of Christ himself. These divine workings of grace are supernatural in so far as they depend upon and actually proceed from the being of God in the person of Christ. At the same time, being historical and formative of history,

---

[181]Ibid., #88,4.

they are natural in so far as they have a general natural connection with the historical life of Christ.[182]

Schleiermacher's belief that Christ is uniquely ordained to communicate the divine power of redemption into our human predicament of sin involves his noted formulation of the two aspects of the redeemer, the *Urbildlichkeit* and the *Vorbildlichkeit*.[183] The *Urbildlichkeit* of Christ is his divine ideality, his personal participation in the power of the divine, which is to be imparted through his perfect God-consciousness to our vitiated God-consciousness. The *Vorbildlichkeit* of Christ, on the other hand, is his human exemplariness, his work of imparting his perfectly submissive world-consciousness as a model for our disproportionate worldliness.

The "ideal" character of Christ is thus the supernatural *power* of redemption, which he combines for us with his "exemplary" character as the natural *model* for redemption. Only because he imparts or communicates *both* to us, however, is he able to serve as God's own agent in the redemption of both our potencies of existence.

Under our condition of sinful world-preoccupation, Christ first communicates to our world-consciousness as the exemplar of how a perfectly submissive world-consciousness must behave. The work of Christ is thus to demonstrate in his model sensible life that sensuous *pleasure* need not be assertive and that sensuous *suffering* need not be evil. Indeed, it is the radical reversal of the ordinary images of sensible pleasure and pain in the model life of Christ which provides the impetus for transforming our own sense-consciousness.

Because Christ's exemplary manifestation of world-consciousness is the correlate of his ideal manifestation of God-consciousness, mankind is effectively brought by him from awareness of the one into awareness of the other. In virtue

---

[182] Ibid., #108,5.

[183] Ibid., #93,2.

of the fact, therefore, that Christ inspires us as the perfect example of human worldliness, he thus concomitantly communicates to us the divine power which determinatively gives to the world power its proper place.

Christ is seen by Schleiermacher as that unique one who overcomes the seemingly unbridgeable gap between supernatural and natural (as in Calvin), or the gap between infinite and finite (as in Kierkegaard), by imparting the infinite within the very terms of the finite. The fact that Christ is the utterly unique agent of God is communicated to us first by his unprecedented reversal of worldly existence, in his active choosing not of pleasure but of suffering, in order then to demonstrate to us what no sinful person could ever see—the proper dominance of God-consciousness over every aspect of world-consciousness.[184]

That Christ should be the redeemer, the unique imparter of grace, is thus a totally unimaginable and inexplicable situation to be presented to the natural human consciousness, for sinful humans gather the mistaken inkling from their struggling God-consciousness that they may within their own existential development come to actualize that power of transcendence that they somehow imagine to be their own. Schleiermacher is very clear in maintaining that the God-consciousness *a se* could never attain to its perfect empowerment from within the process of existence, for God in Christ demonstrates that the universal divine ordination includes much more than a "natural" passage out of sin and into a right relationship with God. It is here that Schleiermacher confounds many of his critics, who find his doctrines too anthropocentric or too mystical, by insisting upon a quite Christocentric doctrine of redemption:

> It is only through [Christ] that the human God-consciousness becomes an existence of God in human nature . . . [because] he alone mediates all existence of God in the world and all revelation of God through the

---

[184]Ibid., #104,2.

world, in so far as he bears within himself the whole new creation which contains and develops the potency of the God-consciousness.[185]

Having understood how Schleiermacher views the definitive and gratuitous role of the redeemer in transforming human existence, we must now consider how the process of redemption is effectively wrought in the respective potencies of actual existence, first in the world-consciousness, and then in the God-consciousness.

The Suppression of World-Consciousness in Grace as the Consciousness of Sin

The transformation that the redeemer effects in the world-consciousness is that which turns it to its foreordained place of submission and subservience to the God-consciousness. In accomplishing this transformation, the power of the *Vorbild* of Christ brings human world-consciousness into the place of God's original intention for it, but the world-consciousness is now also affected by the residual continuance of its past history of sin.

Humanity's world-consciousness, unlike that of Christ, bears the marks of its previous imperfection, and thus of the gracious process by which its imperfection was overcome. "The impression of the sinless perfection of Jesus becomes [for the redeemed] at the same time the complete consciousness *of* sin and the removal of misery."[186]

The implication of this doctrine is that the state of grace makes humans aware both of the natural, ontological continuity of their life in the world, and of the supernatural ingression which assigns their world-consciousness to a new existential role. Only because the redeemer has bridged the gap between supernatural and natural can he effect in us a self-consciousness which "at the

---

[185]Ibid., #94,2.

[186]Ibid., #88,3 (emphasis mine).

same time" comprehends the gravity of its former sin, and comprehends the wonder of the forgiveness of that sin.

Looking back at one's past, as the finite world-consciousness will always do, "it is only from the absolute sinlessness and the perfect spiritual power of the redeemer that we gain the full knowledge of sin."[187] In the former state of sin *per se*, we could have only ethically shaped intimations of our condition, as "consciousness of the law" brought us feelings only of guilt and punishment, but the knowledge of the actual religious context of sin was to be brought to us only in retrospect by the redeemer.

The full significance of the previous state of actual sin is able to be comprehended, however, only because of its radical contrast to the new state of the forgiveness of sin. In the new state itself, the redeemed world-consciousness lives in full comprehension of its former sinful dominance, but also in full acceptance of its gracious reversal:

> Sin in the new man is no longer active [originating]; it is only the after-effect of the old man. The new man thus no longer takes sin to be his own; he indeed labors against it as something foreign to him. The consciousness of guilt [and evils as punishment] is thus abolished. . . . Thus, owing to faith, the consciousness of sin becomes the consciousness of forgiveness of sin.[188]

Since Christians find themselves to have come to a present consciousness of sin only in light of their state of redemption from that sin, it follows for Schleiermacher's hermeneutical logic that only now can Christians truly understand the previous states of original sin and actual sin as necessary precursors to the state of redemption.[189] Unless the states of original sin and actual sin had been fully

---

[187]Ibid., #68,3.

[188]Ibid., #109,2.

[189]Ibid., #66,2.

real stages in the life of human existence, the final state of redemption, in which we have a consciousness *of* sin, would not have been possible. Schleiermacher thus makes clear that "actual sin" is a distinct and separate state of existence from the "consciousness of sin," even though the former provides the setting for the latter:

> In so far as the consciousness of sin is a true element of our existence, and sin therefore a reality, it [sin] is ordained by God as that which makes redemption necessary.[190]

Speaking from the standpoint of the redeemed, Schleiermacher is saying that in so far as one has a forgiven "consciousness of sin" in the state of grace, it must point to a previous state in which "sin" was the reality. In other passages, however, Schleiermacher speaks in less precise terms about "sin" and "consciousness of sin," and this has seemed to many interpreters to indicate that they are equivalent terms, or at least dual aspects of the same state of existence, and not separate states unto themselves. One of the more ambiguous passages of this sort states:

> Sin in general exists only in so far as there is a consciousness of it; and this again is conditioned by a good which must have preceded it and must have been just a result of that original perfection.[191]

This passage is taken by G. N. Boyd to mean that "consciousness of sin" is a function of a type of reflective self-consciousness concurrent with the "sin" in immediate self-consciousness.[192] In keeping with numerous other passages, however, it seems that a clearer understanding of Schleiermacher would indicate

---

[190] Ibid., #81,3.

[191] Ibid., #68,2.

[192] Boyd, "The Doctrine of Original Sin," 47-54 and 64-80.

that "consciousness of sin" is a separate and necessarily contrasting state to "sin" itself, that is, that both are real but *separate* and *successive* states of the actualizing immediate self-consciousness. The passage above thus should probably be taken to mean that "sin in general [actual sin] exists only in so far as there is [successively a state] of consciousness of sin," which is the world-consciousness actualized in a completely different (graceful) state of being.

Schleiermacher does at other times clearly speak of actual sin and consciousness of sin as separate "states,"[193] with the crucial distinction being that in one the world-consciousness ignorantly and blissfully dominates God-consciousness, while in the other the world-consciousness knowingly and painfully submits itself to God-consciousness. As modes of actualization of the world-consciousness, the one clearly must supercede the other, since consciousness-of-sin-as-forgiven could only happen as the opposite of sin-as-committed.

Although in the state of grace we engage in theological and philosophical reflection upon the systematic connection with the previous state of sin, this reflective sort of "consciousness of sin" is quite different for Schleiermacher then the "consciousness of sin" which is the very mode of feeling-existence in world-consciousness during grace. The feeling state of "consciousness of sin" may be a misleading sort of term, but it seems that Schleiermacher clearly saw it as the full state of existence of the world-consciousness as living in light of its forgiven sins, because "owing to faith the consciousness of sin becomes the consciousness of forgiveness of sin."[194]

"With the acceptance of redemption," says Schleiermacher, "there is always conjoined a backward look to sin as prior to it."[195] The acceptance, which is the feeling of God-consciousness in redemption, is conjoined with the feeling of world-consciousness, which must be an inevitable backward look at the

---

[193]Schleiermacher, *The Christian Faith*, #11,3 and #67,2.

[194]Ibid., #109,2.

[195]Ibid., #63,2.

state from which it was redeemed. This backward look is the residuum of sin, or the present "consciousness of sin" even under grace. The state of redemption effects in our world-consciousness "the complete consciousness of sin"—obviously the opposite of sin *per se*—just because redemption has "removed the misery" that attended the actual state.[196]

> We are conscious of [actual] sin as the power and work of a stage when the disposition to the God-consciousness had not yet actively emerged in us.
> In the stage *to which* the consciousness of sin *points back*, sin was not present in us in the same [forgiven] way as we are *now* conscious of it.[197]

The redemption of our world-consciousness is described by Schleiermacher in other places as its "conversion,"[198] so that its relation to the world is converted from a former state to a latter state: "Since without this [state of sin], there could arise no consciousness of sin, the latter is to be understood simply as issuing from the former."[199] While the converted state keeps in mind its present worldly power (forgiveness of sin), it cannot but be aware also of its former worldly power (actual sin). Because the converted state of the world-consciousness is never able to be more than a "consciousness of sin," its characteristic emotion will be pain,[200] at the opposite pole from the pleasure now adhering to the victorious God-consciousness.

The redeemed world-consciousness must always live with a characteristic pain because it is the "consciousness of sin" which always "looks back" with

---

[196]Ibid., #88,3.

[197]Ibid., #67, int. and #67,1 (emphasis mine).

[198]Ibid., #108, int.

[199]Ibid., #68,1.

[200]Ibid., #108,1.

regret at what it enacted before. The "regret" (*Reue*) in the state of consciousness of sin is due to "the retention in consciousness of something that is past."[201] The regret for the sin of the past, along with the forgiveness of sin in the present, combine in the redeemed world-consciousness to produce the "purest and most perfect pain."[202] The *regret* of sin, coming from the fully cognizant *world-consciousness* in the state of redemption, is quite different, says Schleiermacher, from the *guilt* of sin which came previously from the *God-consciousness* in the state of sin, whose pain of sin was induced for reasons that it did not yet understand.

If the role of world-consciousness in the state of grace is essentially that of submission to God-consciousness, and pain at the retention of the old life, how does Schleiermacher explain the Christian's experience that on occasion actual moments of pleasureable world-consciousness will again occur, and assert dominance in actual self-consciousness, so that one will again experience a moment of "actual sin," and not just the consciousness of sin? Schleiermacher suggests that "every Christian is conscious both of sin and grace as always combined with each other"[203] because God has ordained that "sin even in the process of disappearing should continue to exist side by side with grace."[204]

But how, it must be asked, can a reality such as the state of sin exist in Schleiermacher's ontological schema at the same time as another state, the state of grace. The solution, as at least implicitly set out by Schleiermacher, is to demonstrate that what we experience in the state of grace is only varied and separable *moments* of actual sin, but never again the continuous state of sin. If the world-consciousness is able to reassert itself, it will be only in momentary

---

[201] Ibid., #108,2.

[202] Ibid.

[203] Ibid., #64,1.

[204] Ibid., #80,2.

incursions, as "the shadow of sin," without any possibility that it could continuously overcome the definitively empowered God-consciousness. The God-consciousness in the state of grace is always fundamentally in control, and always fundamentally increasing its long-range power.

> The actual sin of those who have been brought into permanent connection with the power of redemption is no longer "originating" in themselves, or through their ill-doing, in others. It has been vanquished by the energy of the God-consciousness implanted in them personally and spontaneously, so that where it still shows itself it is seen to be on the wane, and has no further contaminating power. Hence the sins of the regenerate are such as do not obstruct the spiritual life either in themselves, or in the community.[205]

"The sins of the regenerate" are seen by Schleiermacher to be ordained as those moments that remind us of our past, and of how wondrous it is that the power of grace is that which can redeem us in spite of our finite existential connection to the past. Our sinful moments, says Schleiermacher, are now to be gauged not as potentially dominant tendencies for a renewal of the state of sin, but only as occurring "within the sphere of the Christian consciousness ... by reference to the individual's state of grace."[206]

The state of grace is seen by Schleiermacher, as noted earlier, as a processing state, in which even the special supernatural impartation does not abrogate humanity's basic ontological nature of actualizing existence. The "process of redemption" thus means that people continue to be regenerated and continue to be sanctified, always knowing that they will never escape the threat of their former state of sin. The sins that the regenerate does occasionally commit "will be a basis for the recollection, and to that extent for an actual realization of the old life; and therefore even in moments really involving an advance in likeness

---

[205]Ibid., #74,4.

[206]Ibid., #74,1.

to Christ, there will also exist a consciousness of sin."[207] Even the most "sanctified" individual must always understand that

> As the power of the God-consciousness is never at its absolutely highest any more than the engrafting of the God-consciousness on the excitations of the sensible self-consciousness is ever absolutely constant, there is involved in this circumstance a limiting deficiency of the God-consciousness, which is certainly sinful.[208]

The unique character of a moment of actual sin in the state of grace, however, is that it cannot emerge without its being simultaneously a moment of the consciousness *of* sin, that is, as being an actual sin which yet is accompanied by regret and repentance, and thus covered by the sense of forgiveness.[209] This is why the recurrent moments of sin can have no "originative" or "continuing" effect upon the possibility of other moments of sin, because within the state of grace sin has no present power—only the vestigial power of the past.

This proposition helps to clarify another of the most difficult of Schleiermacher's passages, in which he tells how incidental *actual sins* which still occur in the Christian life must be seen to be subsumed under the simultaneous *consciousness of sin*, which is the general state in which both past and present actual sins are regretted and forgiven.

> Sin cannot emerge in the life of the Christian apart from a consciousness [of it]. To lack this consciousness would simply be an additional sin.
> Within the sphere of Christian piety . . . if in any moment under examination God has formed part of our self-consciousness, but this God-consciousness has not been able to permeate the other [sensible]

---

[207]Ibid., #110,3.

[208]Ibid., #63,3.

[209]Ibid., #108,1 and #111,3.

elements therein, thus determining the moment, then sin and the consciousness of sin are simultaneous.[210]

By so interfusing sin and consciousness of sin in the unique situation of a simultaneous momentary occurrence during the state of redemption, Schleiermacher intimates that the more ordinary occurrence of sin lay in its own mode of actualization in a state simply of "actual sin," previous to the state of "consciousness of sin." This interpretation is reinforced when Schleiermacher goes on to say in the same passage that *most* moments in the state of grace do *not* have a recurrence of actual sin, but have only the consciousness *of* sin in the world-consciousness, which is the ordinary repentant feeling of world-consciousness when under the graceful dominance of God-consciousness.

> Supposing, however, that the God-consciousness has determined the moment, and that pleasure is present in the higher self-consciousness, still every attendant feeling of effort implies a consciousness of sin—in some degree, consequently, annulling that pleasure—since we thereby are made aware that if the sensuous elements which have been overcome had been reinforced form without, the God-consciousness would have been unable to determine the moment.[211]

Schleiermacher seems to be saying that in the state of grace, the Christian will be acutely conscious of sin if actual sin emerges anew, but will basically always live in a general consciousness of sin, for every "feeling of effort" in the now dominant God-consciousness will ever remind this person of the time when actual sin was dominant instead.

The Dominance of God-Consciousness in Grace as the Consciousness of Redemption

Whereas the world-consciousness in the state of grace relates to the *world* in *regret* for its previous assertiveness as sin, the God-consciousness in grace

---

[210]Ibid., #66,1.

[211]Ibid.

relates in *joy* to *God* as the source of the imparted power that overcame sin, and restored the person's God-consciousness to its rightful place. The "joy of fellowship with Christ" is the tone of the redeemed God-consciousness, which as the dominant element in the state of grace now induces the vectorally opposite tone in the dominated world-consciousness, which is the "pain of repentance."[212] The relationship of the two potencies in the actual state of grace is thus rendered in diagram 2.

DIAGRAM 2: CHARACTERISTICS OF GRACE

```
                    WORLD              Consciousness of Sin
  The            CONSCIOUSNESS            (Pain)    (Regret)
                       ↑                           ↑
 State
                    dominates                   induces
                       ↑                           ↑
   of
                     GOD               Consciousness of Redemption
 Grace           CONSCIOUSNESS            (Pleasure)   (Joy)
```

The pleasure, or joy (*Freude*), of the God-consciousness is the emotional tone accompanying its fulfillment, its gratuitous attainment of rightful dominance after being so long suppressed in sin. The tone of joy is the tensile thrust of the continuous strength of the God-consciousness, as it projects its vector of power to induce the opposite tone of pain in the now suppressed world-consciousness.

But because the world-consciousness even as "consciousness of sin" still has the possibility of revitalization, "the [active] shadow of sin,"[213] the dominant power of God-consciousness is ever aware of the redemptive process by

---

[212]Ibid., #108,3.

[213]Ibid., #74,4.

which its joy came to be fulfilled. "The God-consciousness is a joy that passes into humility because its only right to exist is found in what assuages [its former] sorrow lying so near it."[214] Even while it is aware that moments of the old sin may recur, however, the God-consciousness is certain that its new estate is secure, and that no greater kind of joy could be possible than that evinced in the wonder of its salvation.

> Faith gives blessedness [saves], and indeed in such wise that the blessedness cannot be increased from any quarter, i.e., faith *alone* saves.[215]

The "joy of fellowship with Christ," that comes from our participation in his own "blessedness," is of a kind that cannot be derived from any other source, but still it is such as can grow in strength throughout the continuous process of redemption.

> In actual experience the manifestations of the new life become ever more continuous, and that [blessedness] in the endurance of this living union with Christ thus becomes more and more a feature of the actual self-consciousness, for in spite of all fluctuations, an increasing sway of the life of Christ over the flesh marks out the state of sanctification.[216]

Joy, or blessedness (*Seligkeit*), is thus the emotional indicator of the strength of the God-consciousness, *in vectoral relation to* the accompanying suppression of the world-consciousness, which is indicated by its misery (*Unseligkeit*). While the joy of God-consciousness under salvation is the concurrent producer of misery in world-consciousness, it is also the succeeding comparison to the tone of misery that inhered previously in the God-consciousness

---

[214]Ibid., #110,3.

[215]Ibid., #109,4 (emphasis in the original).

[216]Ibid., #111,1.

itself under the state of sin. This retained comparison with its former state is always the reminder of what misery could *temporarily* happen to it again, and of how much grace means as the promise that even such lapses would always be overcome.

> There is always in the God-consciousness, whatever its strength, a blessedness corresponding to that strength; and even in its beginning [of redemption] this blessedness removes the misery [of God-consciousness under sin], though, of course, this can arise again with sin, but only to be again removed.[217]

This joy in the basic strength and continuity of God-consciousness is imparted to us just because we feel it to be forevermore capable of overcoming whatever miserable expressions of sin may reoccur. "Approximations to the condition of blessedness is the real opposite of misery, and this approximation is accepted as divine grace . . . as due to divine agency."[218] The predominance of God-consciousness under grace thus is seen to fit the general pattern of existential progression throughout all the stages of life, for it must always reflect the antithesis of its ontological conjunction with the world-consciousness, even if its power of actualization is felt to be impaired from without.

This situation is explained among the very first theological propositions formulated by Schleiermacher, for he wants to make it clear that the God-consciousness is a natural element of a person's being, even though it receives a supernatural empowerment in its state of piety, or grace.

> The feeling of absolute dependence, even in the realm of redemption, only puts in an appearance, i.e. becomes an actual self-

---

[217]Ibid., #87,1.

[218]Ibid.

> consciousness in time, in so far as it is aroused by a [sensible] determination of consciousness, and unites itself therewith.[219]

As a natural element and as a full participant in the reciprocal conjunction of actual self-consciousness, the God-consciousness is thus always to expect that its dialectical interchange with the opposing world-consciousness will lead it into the antithesis of pleasure and pain.

> What we have thus described [the God-consciousness] constitutes the highest grade of human self-consciousness; but in its actual occurrence it is never separated from the lower [sensible], and through its combination therewith in a single moment it participates in the antithesis of the pleasant and the painful.[220]

"Even in the realm of redemption," the God-consciousness continues its status as an actualized ontological power, now the dominant one, and thus stands at that end of the vectoral antithesis of pleasure and pain. It is only in this "ultimate" state of its empowerment, moreover, that it finally comprehends its true nature, and sees the process of existential dialectic through which it has passed on the way to being redeemed. The fact that redemption empowers a "communicated facility"[221] to the God-consciousness does not mean that the God-consciousness ceases to be a human capacity, still involved in recollecting toward its past, and actualizing in its present, the antithesis of pleasure and pain.

> In this [redemption] as in other stages of experience, pleasure and pain are by no means to be regarded as so separate from each other that one

---

[219]Ibid., #30,1.

[220]Ibid., #5, int.

[221]Ibid., #63,2.

of them might in some circumstances actually exist without the other.[222]

The God-consciousness, even in the state of redemption, thus occurs like the finite potency it is, "as the actual content of a moment of experience only under the general form of self-consciousness, that is, the antithesis of pleasure and pain."[223]

The God-consciousness does find a unique empowerment in the state of grace, but it nonetheless finds itself to be the same finite human capacity it has always been only now fully cognizant of the existential struggle with which it is imprinted, but which it may now have confidence that it has been enabled to win.

---

[222]Ibid., #62,1.

[223]Ibid., #62, int.

CHAPTER 4

CONCLUDING EVALUATION: THE PLACE OF THE DOCTRINE OF SIN IN SCHLEIERMACHER'S SYSTEM OF THOUGHT

INTRODUCTION

The issue of the significance of sin in Schleiermacher's thought can now be seen to involve both his theological program, as epitomized in *The Christian Faith*, and his philosophical program, as epitomized in the *Dialectic*. The connections between his philosophy and his theology may ultimately be seen to manifest a dialectical interdependence, if not a continuity, of both, and the doctrine of sin can serve as an apt illustration of how the philosophical backdrop is formally necessary for the theological explication.

The principle of "dialectic" indeed may be taken as a common critical category of both philosophical and theological explanation for Schleiermacher. The dialectic that characterizes all of being includes the essence and the existence of human beings, and is found to be actually manifested first in human sin, where it is the reciprocating struggle for domination between God-consciousness and world-consciousness in the formative moments and states of existence. By the same token, moreover, dialectical reciprocity is found also in the moments and states of grace, in which the God-consciousness still must strive to maintain its dominance over world-consciousness. The important point, therefore, is that "reciprocal dialectic" is a principle of operation *within* the ontological sphere of human relativity, and not a metaphysical nexus between the sphere of absoluteness and the sphere of relativity.

The "absolute one" is that for Schleiermacher which determines the entire concatenation of being to lie in dialectical relativity, but which is itself entirely non-dialectical or non-relational in its activity of determination. Any dialectic that humans may imagine to obtain between God and the world is in reality only the mediating dialectic *within* human self-conscious actualization of the two, as the human seeks to conjoin the sources of one's self-consciousness, of being determined both by God and by the world. Humans are indubitably self-conscious of being absolutely determined by God, but that self-consciousness operates only as one factor in human existence, set into reciprocal conjunction with world-consciousness, in the dialectical struggle for continuing actualization.

The basic dialectic that obtains within the ontological sphere of human existence is thus the reciprocal conjunction of the two potencies of self-conscious existence. It is further extended in the dialectic of existential process, in which the two potencies' struggle for dominant actualization goes through the states of sin and grace. The dialectic is thus completely located within the ontological structure and existential process of human feeling, and must be understood as the human person's "free" response to the two potencies that the person receives as determined from without.

The truth that theology comprehends from the completed dialectic of existential process, which philosophy could not formerly comprehend simply from the original dialectic of ontological structure, is that the dialectic of human existence, that is, both the structure *and* process of conjuctive actualization of potencies, is set up within the person by the absolute divine determination. The dialectic of human existence is in Schleiermacher's view absolutely determined to follow the process of sin and grace, or of creation and redemption, in a continuous way. This disallows any supposition that God accomplishes a transcendentally dialectical incursion into the life of human existence, such as a program of radical revelation or redemption would entail.

For Schleiermacher, instead, the occurrence of redemption is the dialectical reciprocate of creation which precedes it, since both are posited within the intrinsic scope of existence, yet both are parts of an extrinsic determination by the absolute. Indeed, Schleiermacher seems to say that if creation and redemption are dialectical poles in the outworking of existence, then sin and grace must also be dialectically related. As a result of his theological insight that the final existential stage of redemption, or grace, is possible only because of the sinful tendency of original creation, Schleiermacher seems willing to see the entire dialectic of sin and grace as the single ultimate decree of the one absolute God.[1]

The question of divine determination versus human responsibility thus devolves into the question of how human freedom functions as the dialectical process of existential self-actualization, while still being under the determinative structure of existence as set out by God. Mankind is fated to freedom, but in Schleiermacher's revision of the tragic outlook, the final fate that freedom actualizes is a wholly good one, even though that existential freedom has come to mankind as a real struggle. Human fate is secure, but our freedom must follow the actual feelings of dialectical struggle between the potencies of God-feeling and world-feeling. The reciprocal interchange between the two indelibly marks each with some qualities of the other, thereby assuring that the dialectic within existence will never be overcome within its own terms.

The dialectical conjunction of God-consciousness and world-consciousness within every moment and state of actual existence means that the two potencies do have a real degree of reciprocal influence upon one another therein. In the actual state of sin, that influence means that the dominant world-feeling (of relative multiplicity) colors the conjoined but recessive feeling of an absolute unity. In the state of grace, however, the clarifying dominance of God-conscious-

---

[1]Schleiermacher, *The Christian Faith*, #94,3.

ness influences our consciousness of the world, making it known that the source of that dialectically reciprocating feeling of absoluteness has indeed been responsible for the total dialectic having turned out as it has. The state of grace, Schleiermacher would say, allows one to say with theological insight that the dialectical process of existence has been the progressive exercise of the divine will in revealing to humans both the priority and the finality of its absolute power over them.

For Schleiermacher it is clear that God is the absolute one who does not participate in dialectical interchange, but who rather posits it in all of being: in the *essential* breadth of being, which is the co-inherent (*Ineinandersein*)[2] dialectic of real and ideal, and in humanity's particular *existential* being, which is the reciprocal (*Wechselwirkung*)[3] dialectic of God-consciousness and world-consciousness. All of being has its nature and its history as a type of interrelated dialectic of polar factors, but all of it is found to be determined in this way by the unitary absolute. The absolute stands beyond the dialectic of nature and history, beyond the dialectic of creation and redemption, and can in no sense be found as immanent within, or as even related to, either of the terms of the dialectic.

Schleiermacher would thus deny the neo-orthodox view of a specific dialectical relationship of God to history, just as he would deny a Spinozistic view of a specific dialectical relationship of God to nature. Further, he would deny any Hegelian sort of emanational or idealistic view of God as the dialectical source and sum of both history and nature together. Clearly, he intends to affirm a view of an absolutely transcendent God who simply commands (*gebietet*) and effects (*hervorbringt*) a dialectical concourse of being, which fulfills itself on its own terms and then is willfully remanded back to the one.

In the human quest for understanding, however, we must begin our efforts to affirm the infinite one by comprehending and affirming the infinitely

---

[2]Braun & Bauer, II, *Ethik,* 248.

[3]Schleiermacher, *The Christian Faith,* #4,2.

determined finite relativity of our existence, by "feeling" both poles of the dialectical forces within the self. Humans can only vaguely ascertain the dimensions of the two forces that determine the self, however, and Schleiermacher realizes that a person must always start with one or the other pole of the self-consciousness in order to understand their dialectical structure and process. The question is that of with which pole the individual may start.

THE STARTING POINT OF DIALECTICAL UNDERSTANDING: CREATION OR REDEMPTION

Because the dialectic that Schleiermacher ascertains is a dialectic *within* human existence, the hermeneutical process of understanding existence must involve a process of explicating the terms of the dialectic, with a criterion established for deciding which term is more basic. Should one begin with the world-consciousness or the God-consciousness, since both are formally co-equal as components of the structure of actual self-consciousness? Or should one begin with the world-dominant phase or the God-dominant phase, since both are equally real stages in the existential process of that self-consciousness? Or is there a more comprehensive dialectic between the structure of existence and the process of existence, which must itself be analyzed?

Schleiermacher does seem to suggest that the ultimate dialectic within human life is that between the foundational structures of existence (creation) and the operational process of existence (redemption). In traditional terms, the hermeneutical issue then becomes whether we understand the whole dialectic of existence better if we start with its structure (philosophy), or if we start with its process (theology). Although there is a clear necessity that both be included, and that both contribute reciprocally to the understanding of the other, still Schleiermacher seems ultimately to affirm that the theological standpoint of redemption-process is what provides the insight by which the structure of creation can best be understood.

Nevertheless, even though the process of existence provides the fuller insight than does the structure of existence, Schleiermacher is careful to follow the inner dialectical workings of both the structure (between world-consciousness and God-consciousness) and the process (between the stages of world-dominant sin and of God-dominant grace). For the totality of human self-understanding, Schleiermacher seems to say, we must have the complementary working of philosophical ontology and theological phenomenology. Only when both the being and the becoming of human existence are considered together, therefore, can we hope to see the overall dialectical composition of human existence, as it is determined for us by the absolute.

In various places, therefore, Schleiermacher seems to step back and to point out his hermeneutical approach, of combining the two understandings of existence into a dialectical whole. In outlining his two-pronged effort for *The Christian Faith*, he states:

> We shall exhaust the whole compass of Christian doctrine if we consider the facts of the religious self-consciousness, first, as they are presupposed [in the ontology of created existence] by the antithesis expressed in the concept of redemption, and secondly, as they are determined [in the theology of redeemed existence] by the antithesis.[4]

The necessity of looking together at the ontological structure of creation and at the theological processes of redemption is granted because both are found ultimately to be under a unified divine determination.

> The decree that sent Christ forth is one with the decree creating the human race, for in Christ first human nature is brought to perfection.[5]

---

[4]Ibid., #29, int.

[5]Ibid., #109,3.

Schleiermacher thus clearly changes the traditional hiatus between creation and redemption into a dialectical reciprocity, and in the supposition of its absolute determination, into an outright continuous whole. What is known about the structures of created existence provides the only possible context for understanding redemption; on the other hand, what is known in the process of redeemed existence provides the final interpretation of the original creation. Neither the incompleteness of creation nor the completeness of redemption is designed just for the sake of the other, but both are rather to be seen as continuous factors in the effecting of God's overall will.

> Christ therefore was determined as he was, only because, and in so far as, everything as a whole was determined in a certain way; and conversely, everything as a whole was only so determined, because, and in so far as, Christ was determined in a certain way. To say this is obviously to take our stand upon the divine good-pleasure (*Wohlgefallen*), and to say that the determination [*Bestimmung*] in both cases is what it is simply through the divine good-pleasure.[6]

Even though both aspects of existence are developmentally necessary to the full actualization of human potential, it is still Schleiermacher's intention to uphold redemption as the relatively superior, and complete, aspect of existential actualization. The fundamental structures of created existence are found to harbor the locus and the origin of sin, and in this sense creation must be reckoned as at the least in a relative-dialectical inferiority to redemption. But the imperfect context of sinfully preoccupied created existence, even in its limited philosophical self-understanding, still points by dialectical implication toward the finally redeemed existence which it denies. The sin implicit in creation fervently seeks the *actuality* of redemption in the process of existence, and does not merely wonder about a *possibility* of redemption from the static structures of existence.

---

[6] Ibid., #120,3.

The reason that the process of redemption gives a person the more incisive and more complete view of oneself than could have been gained just from one's status in creation, is that in redemption one understands the *existenziell* concreteness of one's life before the absolute God, whereas in creation the person could understand only the *existenzial* generality of life as issuing from a misconstrued ontological structure of relative identity. The self-concept suggested by philosophical ontology is the necessary general framework for any understanding of oneself, but that concept will be seen by theology to have been limited in its comprehension of how the given structures of existence become misaligned into the configuration of sin.

Only from the perspective of theologically understood redemption will the created structures of selfhood be fully comprehended in their proper alignment, for only the clarifying dominance of God-consciousness is able to reveal to the self the meaning of the redemption which has been wrought from creation. It is this grasp of the pervasive significance of redemption in the dialectic of human life which led Schleiermacher in his last lectures on hermeneutics to affirm that theological interpretation should be the crux and arbiter of all philosophical approaches to the interpretation of humankind.[7]

Theology of course is still dependent upon and receptive to the insights of philosophy, but the specific existential (*existenziell*) stance of redemption perceives that in it is embodied the definitive truth of human existence, which the original creation had only implied and sought after. Creation thus could not contain within it a complete system of self-understanding, which an ontological-existential hermeneutic like that of Schubert Ogden would suppose, but neither would it be radically divorced from the redemption to come, as in the revelational hermeneutic of neo-orthodoxy. Schleiermacher would probably not even affirm such a hermeneutic as that of paradoxical dialectic found in Bultmann, for Schleiermacher believed that creation and redemption clearly and determinatively involved one

---

[7]Schleiermacher, *Sämmtliche Werke*, I/7, *Hermeneutik*, 262.

another, in a reciprocal dialectic seen finally by redemption to be one of ordained development.

That the process of human redemption is the dialectical fulfillment of our created structure is evident to theology, not because God dialectically reveals a cognitive apprehension of the fact, but because the God-consciousness structurally posited in creation has now been brought by its own power to its proper place of dominance in the continuing human existence. The earlier struggles in the process of self-actualization can now be termed as sin, for in them humans disallowed the urges toward empowerment by the suppressed God-consciousness. Only in redemption can sin be fully understood in its dialectical opposition, and also fully relegated to its true status as a necessarily and negatively actualized foil to redemption.

> As regards the divine attributes, it is of course evident that statements concerning God cannot issue from a condition of alienation from God, but are only possible when a man is in some sense turned again toward him. But not even where sin is viewed from the standpoint of a paramount God-consciousness can we conceive of divine attributes that have to do with sin apart from its disappearance as a result of redemption.[8]

Only in the realm of redemption is a person able to understand how serious was the realm of sin which preceded it, but which can now also be seen as the necessary foundation for the eventuation of redemption. The created structures of human existence are seen by redemption to have been determinately misaligned, so that the process of divine ordination could bring them back into their properly related status.

> It has been well-pleasing to God that human nature should show itself in this determined multiplicity of thus determined human beings. . . .

---

[8]Schleiermacher, *The Christian Faith*, #64,2.

> Similarly, it has been his good-pleasure to make the dispensation of human affairs perfect through Christ.[9]

For Schleiermacher, the redemption of human existence provides the better hermeneutical starting-point than does the creation, for only redemption understands the total scope of human existence from the stage of supremacy of the God-consciousness, and in this is manifested the absolute determination of the overall dialectic by which creation is rendered into redemption.

> For the pious, there is no path of escape from this circle of necessities, each leading back to and conditioned by the others, except by way of this one all-inclusive divine good-pleasure. Accordingly, all that remains to us is the task of linking up at every point this divine good-pleasure (which is necessarily implicit in our God-consciousness) with what we perceive of the actual course of the work of redemption, and of resting trustfully upon it, however we may be moved by what happens.[10]

When the theology of redemption is thus superimposed upon the philosophy of creation, Schleiermacher is at times led to shift into a third mode of discourse, which views the dialectical relativity of human existence *qua* under the determinative aegis of the absolute, and this "transcendental" mode of discourse is what Schleiermacher designates as the "philosophy of religion."

DETERMINISM AND FREEDOM: HOW SCHLEIERMACHER'S SYSTEM LOGICALLY ENTAILS SIN

A certain dialectic of reciprocity is found by Schleiermacher to obtain respectively within each aspect of human existence, within both the elemental structure of existence and the developmental process of existence. Within the

---

[9]Ibid., #120,3.

[10]Ibid.

elemental *structure* of existence is found the ontological dialectic between God-consciousness and world-consciousness, the dialectical conjunction of which is actual self-consciousness. Within the consequent *process* of existence is found the existential dialectic of the stages of sin and grace, in which the elemental potencies arrange themselves into differing patterns of actual dominance. The principle that functions as the common dialectical synthesis of *both* aspects of existence is thus the "actual self-consciousness," for it is seen by Schleiermacher as that permanent *structural* focus by which existence becomes a *process*, by which the person's being continually enters into the becoming of its stages.

Actual self-consciousness (feeling) is therefore for Schleiermacher the central reality of human existence, whose ever-continuous transposition from ontological structure into teleological process provides the evidence of an absolutely unitary non-dialectical determination of the dialectic itself. The actual self-consciousness is the person's existence-freedom, but it is found to entail the existential freedom precisely of "feeling" the dialectic into which a person is determined. Actual self-consciousness is the realization of one's posited *structure* of existence through the development of one's posited *process* of existence, and the "freely" appropriated dialectic of both together is found to be posited as a complete and absolute determination. The absolute determination is indeed the only possible explanation of the teleological tension that appears to humans from within the dialectic itself.

What a person perceives from the creation side of one's existence (ontology) is the dialectic as antithetical, and it is only from the subsequent redemption side of existence (theology) that one can see the dialectic to have been actually reciprocal, and therefore as teleologically oriented by an absolutely external source of its internal dialectical determinancy. It is in so conceiving of an utterly transcendent principle of absolute determination that Schleiermacher is able to give an ultimate logical consistency to his system, and to explain the human freedom of dialectical self-actualization as being totally the appointed will of the unitary absolute.

Many interpreters of Schleiermacher have found less than a systematic consistency within his thought, however, and have offered the kind of critique presented by Gerhard Spiegler in *The Eternal Covenant*.[11] This line of criticism sees Schleiermacher as caught in the inconsistency of assuming an absolutely non-dialectical God, who yet is involved in a dialectical interchange, or covenant, with humankind. This sort of critique seems to assume, however, that Schleiermacher believes God to be actually disposed within the human consciousness of God, within the consciousness of absolute dependence.

Such a line of interpretation disregards the consistently held axiom of Schleiermacher that the human existential feeling of God is referential, intentional, or teleological, and not ontologistic in any sense. Indeed, this theological axiom must be reflected back into the philosophical theories of mankind's tentative search for a principle of absoluteness within the dialectic of existence *per se*. When this is done, it becomes clear that in both departments of his thought Schleiermacher suggests that the human God-consciousness, or the consciousness of the absolute, functions only as a relative factor in the dialectical context of existence, as a dialectical participant in both its structure and its process.

Indeed, it is only because the God-consciousness is determined by God to be at the disposal of a person's existential freedom that sin can and does occur. Not only is the God-consciousness determined together with world-consciousness as the two posited potentials of the *structure* of existence, but the God-consciousness is also determined to go with world-consciousness through the *process* of existence, from being blocked to being opened—from sin to grace. Such an affirmation of the absolute determinancy of the person's relative dialectical existence is what anchors for Schleiermacher the logical consistency of the entire system of thought.

The purview of absolute determination is still a "transcendental" projection from the person's existentially relative position, but the existential status of

---

[11]Gerhard Spiegler, *The Eternal Covenant* (New York: Harper & Row, 1967).

redemption is that phenomenologically clarified status in which the person finally is given the certain apprehension of the absolute *otherness* of the source of one's feeling of absolute dependence, and thus the apprehension of the absolute determination of the self and all else. Schleiermacher is not, therefore, offering a theodicy *sub specie aeternitatis*, but is simply affirming in a philosophy-of-religion way that whatever humans do know (philosophically) from their relative (religious) experience of sin and grace must be accounted to that one who determines humans to know him only *qua* the absolute source of all determination.[12]

Only from the standpoint of redemption, however, do humans find that they are granted to know even that there *is* one all-determinative "commanding will" of God, and not just the dialectically "efficient will" that is all that they could grasp before. From the human standpoint, redemption does further enable humans to affirm that the entire teleological dialectic of creation-redemption within existence points beyond itself, beyond just the efficiently structured process to a determinative source of command standing absolutely beyond it.

Mankind can never know, even from redemption, *what* the universally commanded will of God entails, but redemption does for the first time allow the person to "feel" *that* the commanded will is there, as the source of the absolutely efficient will. One's comprehension of the absolute transcendence of God's commanding will is thus given to the person only as one's feeling of absolute dependence upon it. This feeling, moreover, is itself never purely apprehended, but is always admixed with the world feeling, so that the commanding will of God is adumbrated for the person only as the efficient will carrying out the dialectic of creation and redemption.

Schleiermacher's most critical assumption, therefore, is that the phenomenological intentionality in the feeling of the absolute dependence of one's entire existence does indeed refer to a transcendent metaphysical principle of absolute determination. On the basis of this assumption, Schleiermacher can explicate a

---

[12]Schleiermacher, *The Christian Faith*, #81,4.

systematic coherence throughout the whole spectrum of his thought, for all the dialectical polarities of humankind and of the world may be seen as but relative effects of a single, non-dialectical determinant.

The key issue, therefore, becomes whether or not the human *feeling* of absolute dependence is an adequate demonstration that such an absolute principle allows itself to be even relatively comprehended. Does a person's phenomenological comprehension of the dialectic in existence, whereby the feeling of absolute dependence is effected into final dominance and clarity, actually reveal a transcendent source of commanded determination behind those dialectical operations? This question of the ontological and epistemological content of "feeling" may certainly be raised by critical viewpoints external to Schleiermacher's system. From within the system, however, there is no doubt that the dialectical nature of feeling-existence is logically coherent with the unitary nature of the absolute principle by which it is determined.

FEELING AS FREEDOM: ITS CONCEPTUAL ADEQUACY IN A DETERMINISTIC SYSTEM

The issue of the internal consistency that Schleiermacher manifests in his view of dialectically actualized determinism becomes problematic mainly in reference to the place of human existence, in which the dialectic of actual self-consciousness presents itself as being free, as well as being determined. The extent to which humans do self-consciously or freely determine their own feelings, is the extent to which they may doubt that the reciprocity within them is determined by an absolute source from beyond. But the extent to which humans also perceive a total, external causality as unilaterally revealing itself through one aspect of their feelings is the extent to which they may finally believe their "free" feelings to have been categorically determined.

The traditional conservative line of criticism of Schleiermacher's concept of "feeling" finds that feeling is too subjectivistic, too involved in the immediacy of its self-apprehension. This study has suggested, however, that the true nature of feeling is quite different, for in it Schleiermacher seeks to locate humanity's existentially actualized response to the objective realms of world and God that come to us as determining our essential being. Any critique that might be made of "feeling," therefore, should rather find it *too* objectivistic, referential, impersonal, or determined really to serve as a designation for the heart of humanity's free personal existence.

The emphasis in Schleiermacher's definition of feeling is upon the self's dialectical responsiveness to its sources of determination, world and God, which present themselves as the two definitively objective potencies that humans must "freely" actualize in their existence of feeling. "Existence" for Schleiermacher is the person's standing out of the two potencies that determine the person, the one relatively and the other absolutely. The feeling of "freedom" in existence is therefore the person's capacity to actualize one's world context more easily than one's God context, but this freedom is felt indeed only up to the point in which the person becomes reoriented to the actualization of one's absolute determination from God.

The reorientation of human existence is finally perceived not to have been the work of one's own actualizing capacity, but to have been capacitated or empowered within one by the source of absolute determination, which thereby manifests its nature into the person's own relative nature. *Sola gratia* indeed becomes the watchword even of the existential process of human feelings, and *sola fide* is rejected because it would allow too much free capacity to the self-actualizing, rather than to the potencies that are determined to be actualized.

The richness of the existential paradox of freedom-within-fate is strongly tilted toward Schleiermacher's controlling supposition that absolute determination defines both the structure and the process of human freedom. The existence of freedom in such a context is what constitutes for Schleiermacher the life of "feeling," but the rich intensity of subjectively personal awareness is what seems in many ways to be vitiated by the objective intentionality and ultimate determinability of all feeling. Even though Schleiermacher does affirm that while the person is caught within the domination of the relatively free world-consciousness one feels oneself to be free, the person nonetheless is ultimately brought to the graceful state of ascertaining that the given dialectic and paradox in all of existence is relative to an absolute determination.

The person's feeling, or the process of one's actual existence, will always continue in its dialectical relativity, but its climactic stage with the graceful assertion of God-consciousness provides one with the realization that the entire life of feeling has been calibrated and oriented by a source absolutely beyond it. This reflection of the program of absolute determination upon the person's putatively free feeling is what infuses Schleiermacher's view of feeling with a sense of hardness and exactitude quite unlike the usual interpretation that human feeling is freely self-indulgent and vague. Indeed, the real problem for Schleiermacher may be that his critical principle of absolute determination renders the human nature of feeling, or immediate self-consciousness, only an existential gloss upon the dialectic of essential being, which is fully directed by the absolute will. If a monism of absolute will is the originative source of reality, then the dialectic of human feeling must be the directed response to it, quite lacking in the subtle and sentimental aspects usually attributed to feeling.

Whether Schleiermacher fully realizes that his view of feeling inevitably becomes colored by the transcendental dominance of an impersonal causality is difficult to ascertain, since he does in many instances attempt to portray the free deliberations of feeling as being affectively influenced by one or another of its objects. This somewhat romantic version of feeling is usually mitigated, however, by the ever-surrounding sense that even the affectivity is a function of a basically impersonal self which is existing primarily to reflect the non-affectively posited determinations of the self. What results, in light of Schleiermacher's deterministic system, is such an absolutely impersonal God that the human, too, in the image of God, comes to exist as a being whose unique capacity of "feeling" its determinations is also impersonally rendered.

Feeling is seen by Schleiermacher as that dialectical position at the heart of every human whereby a person exposits (existentializes) the two determinations that conjointly posit (essentialize) the self. In being so "posited" as "expositing," the human existential feeling, or actual self-consciousness, is that which actualizes the two contrasting potentials from world and God. The human as an actualizer is the concrete agent, the operant mediator, determined as standing between and as conjoining its two determinations.

The human being exists, therefore, as an actual self-consciousness, a feeling agent, whose agency works both ontologically and epistemologically to mediate and to exposit its conjoining determinations. In this regard, feeling must be seen for Schleiermacher not as an amorphous self-indulgence, but as a concrete agency existentially actualizing the two determinative realities that constitute its entire potential. Feeling is not, therefore, an immediacy of ontologistic participation in the external determinations, but rather is the *immediate* consciousness of the self *qua* existentially *mediating* the two determinations, which always lie beyond the self that they determine.

Feeling is defined as the basic nature of the human being because in it a person relatively apprehends, somewhat ontologically and somewhat epistemologically, the determinations that control humanity. Human feeling is given us so that we may "be" and may "know" in relation to the determinants, as we exist out of them. This position of feeling-existence is the person's total possibility, so that the actualization of it is one's appointed good, and it is therefore quite unlike the frustrating Sartian-type existence in which humans are only confused by their effort both to be and to know. The human being's existence is good, because in it a person actualizes one's position of dialectical mediation between the two potentiating determinations, and affirms the absolute dominance of the one determinant in regard to the other, and also in regard to oneself as the creature of both.

The human being's existence-feeling is not only good, says Schleiermacher, but it is also real, for it involves the total disposition of the person by the only two dimensions of reality, the relative world and the absolute divine. Human feeling is the person's unique mode of involvement with reality, for in it one finds represented the two real determinants of one's essential self, the distinctly non-dialectical realities of God and world, *as if* they were dialectically conjoined in the actuality of the human feeling of them. The traditional critique of Schleiermacher's "feeling," that it is too ephemeral and psychologistically experiential, must surely be corrected by the affirmation that feeling is the distinctly human dimension of reality because it enables the self to be posited by the distinct realities beyond it.

If feeling is neither fanciful nor free for Schleiermacher, but rather is basically real and basically determined, then both its aspects (creation and redemption) must be seen in turn to be quite real and quite determined. Indeed, it is only because the affective freedom of feeling is so subsumed into the overall impersonal determinism that Schleiermacher is able to display both the creation and the redemption of feeling-humanity as dialectical aspects of the person's absolute determination. In this light, both sin and grace are to be seen as seriously real, because they are respective states of human feeling-existence, and are thus dialectically ordained as the disposition of human reality.

> Sin is referred to that highest degree of inward activity [feeling] which constitutes the distinctive element in our being. What then is here asserted is that in the whole process of life . . . free self-actualization is always attended by sin.
> Hence, if this whole form of existence subsists in virtue of divine appointment, sin, as proceeding from human freedom, has also a place in that appointment.[13]

But the "free" activation of sin is no less determined than the imparted activation of grace, and both states of life are thus seen as fully real, only because both are fully and correlatively determined.

---

[13]Ibid., #81,2.

> In so far as the consciousness of our sin is a true element of our being, and sin therefore a reality, it is ordained by God as that which makes redemption necessary.
>
> By the commanding will of God, accordingly, sin has been ordained by God, not indeed sin in and of itself, but sin merely in relation to redemption; for otherwise redemption itself could not have been ordained.[14]

The crucial problem with Schleiermacher's understanding of human feeling thus seems to be that it must be located in a relative realm of never-ending dialectical existence, but that it must exposit a non-dialectical conjunction of relative world and absolute God which together constitute its essential determination. The concept of feeling, or the free actualization within human existence, is therefore systematically overwhelmed by the logical priority of absolute determination in Schleiermacher's thinking. It finds its given position of dialectically mediating world-consciousness and God-consciousness, creation and redemption, and sin and grace, as a position whose freedom and affection for its constituents are overborne completely by the reality of absolute determination. The only way, therefore, in which human existence can be granted the dignity, freedom, affection, and reality which its systematic context denies it, is in Schleiermacher's designation of Christ as the uniquely determining empowerment of human potentials into perfect actualization.

THE PERFECT DETERMINATION OF ACTUAL SELF-CONSCIOUSNESS IN CHRIST

Although Schleiermacher's system of thought might basically be understood as the dialectical interchange between the philosophy of human freedom and the theology of human determination, the deficiencies within the philosophical concept of feeling-as-freedom have been seen to be glaring enough

---

[14]Ibid., #81,3.

to suggest why Schleiermacher uses the theological concept of the redeemer to explain the determined perfecting of human feeling. As the divinely ordained mediator, Christ determines in human terms the perfection of the dialectical actualization in feeling that no other could possibly embody. Only he perfectly conveys the propriety of absolute determinism within human freedom, and thereby becomes the concrete agent whereby every other human being may be brought into a redemptive re-creation of its concrete existence.

The proper existence of humanity is redeemed out of its creation only by Christ, for his role as mediator is that determined by God to impart to humans the capacity of true freedom. Within the personhood of Christ, God determines that human consciousness of the absolute and consciousness of the world are for the first time to be proportionately conjoined, and thereby that Christ should inspire and empower other people into similar states of harmony. Christ enables everyone to find in their feelings of free self-actualization a sense of affection and intention which sheer determination might otherwise have wrung out of them. The personal Christ, in Schleiermacher's view, serves to bridge the gap between the awesome severity of absolute determination and the experienced struggle of human freedom.

Christ reaches people, and brings our redemption out of our creation, because Christ, too, is determined as a concrete existent who feels the power of both God-consciousness and world-consciousness, but who is not determined to misappropriate their given dialectical relation. Christ demonstrates and enables us to know that human existence (feeling) is the ultimate concrete position of dialectically conjoining the realm of the transcendent and the realm of the immanent. The person's own feeling is the ultimate concretion and ultimate mediacy within being, and one thus need look no further than to Christ, the perfect feeling-being, to encounter God's sovereign will for humanity mediated in concrete form.

The hermeneutical problem of starting point is thus resolved in the manifestation of Christ as the medium in which the transcendent becomes immanent, the divine becomes worldly, and the absolute becomes concrete. A person need look no further than to the perfect human to discover the conjunction of model (*Vorbild*) and power (*Urbild*) for the redemption of one's misconjoined world-consciousness and God-consciousness.[15] The divine *logos* is the mediator ordained by the absolute into concrete form, so that his sensible *logos* might first appeal to human world-consciousness, lost in sin, in order then that the spiritual *logos* might appeal to human God-consciousness, and bring it into grace.

The *logos* of Christ is thus God's determination that the dialectic of spirit and flesh should at last be perfect—that their conjunction in every person need not always be a confusion or paradox, but should rather be the total actualization of God's will for human life. Christ breaks the confusion between active sin and passive suffering[16] in order to appeal to human *world-consciousness*, and in so doing he empowers human *God-consciousness* into its proper ascendancy over the worldly side.

Even though no other will ever attain the perfection granted to Christ, nonetheless the state of redemption granted to the ordinary person will involve the clear dominance of God-consciousness over world-consciousness, and the sense that one's very existence is now recreated by an absolute determination whose manifestation is both personal and real. The antinomy between determinism and freedom is overcome only in the existence of Christ, and through him humans discover the singular meaning of freedom in feeling, the personalization of existence which sheer divine determinism would otherwise mysteriously obscure.

God's determination of our freedom is really comprehended, and indeed enjoyed, only in the state of redemption, in which Christ reveals God's final will for the entire plan of human existence, from creation to redemption. The *commanded* will of God is then seen to be absolutely beyond the dialectic of human existence, but yet to have been executed as the *efficient* will of God in the mediation of Christ. Christ is therefore the unique agent in Schleiermacher's

---

[15]Ibid., #93,2.

[16]Ibid., #104,2.

conceptual system whereby the absolute determination of God wills itself to be made the relative determination of the dialectic of human existence. This conceptualization of Christ helps to tighten Schleiermacher's internal logic of absolute determinism in regard to human freedom, but more than this, it also augments the concept of human freedom, or feeling-existence, with aspects of affectiveness and gracefulness which are lacking without the presence of Christ.

The incoming presence of the perfect existence of Christ as the power of redemption may seem to the redeemed human existence to be a supernatural incursion into our natural, or created, state. Such a view as that of dialectical theology thus would hold that redemption is a radical dialectic between the absolute one and the relative person, but Schleiermacher points out that fuller insight into the mediation of Christ reveals that he is the agent by which divine determination is effected as a dialectic *within* human existence *per se*. The dialectic between creation and redemption might at first seem to the redeemed to be a radical discontinuity within his existence, but the mediating role of Christ finally is understood to have brought about the redemption of the original creation, the completion of a continuous internally dialectical plan effected by the external command of the divine.

Christ is the concrete figure who embodies and effects the fullness of redemption out of created human existence, and who thereby makes our own existence transpire as the concrete dialectic of the two stages. From a human perspective, however, the dialectic is so mysterious and so pronounced that one is always tempted to view it as a radically immediate manifestation of divine power, rather than as a re-manifestation of the mediated feeling of God which has only been temporarily obscured. Our human perspective will thus always be imperfectly limited to our experiential actualization in the dialectic, and only through faith in the word of Christ may we comprehend the perfect continuity and unity which God has determined to be effected through dialectical means.

Christ reveals to us that "he was determined as he was, only because, and in so far as, everything as a whole was determined in a certain way,"[17] and redemption becomes the telescope through which creation is understood and combined with it as the dialectically effected will of God.

> There is only one eternal and universal decree justifying men for Christ's sake . . . The decree that sent Christ forth is one with the decree creating the human race, for in Christ first human nature is brought to perfection.[18]

In Schleiermacher's view, only through actual, concrete faith in the actual, concrete Christ can a person "feel" beyond both the philosophically and theologically conceived ambiguities of one's existential dialectic, and believe that Christ has been appointed by the absolute to mediate to us a fuller actualization of that absolute determination which we only relatively receive.

Christ concretely establishes the finite dialectical distance between sin and grace, as he embodies for everyone the grace of sinless self-consciousness, yet he also overcomes that distance by revealing the infinite determinancy that has brought the dialectic to completion. The true nature and reality of sin are able to be known only because Christ demonstrates to redeemed people how distant was their former state from the piety that grace empowers them to attain. A complete doctrine of sin for Schleiermacher is thus able to be ascertained only when the doctrine of piety is clearly apprehended, but the full comprehension of the implications of sin can in return further illuminate the dialectical reciprocity that has led to grace. A combined philosophical-theological perspective, according to Schleiermacher, enables us to see the relative differences and relative similarities of the states of sin and grace, but it also enables us to understand that the purely theological perspective of grace contains whatever revelation of absolute truth is given to humans to know.

---

[17]Ibid., #120,3.

[18]Ibid., #109,3.

SELECTED BIBLIOGRAPHY

I. PRIMARY SOURCES

Schleiermacher, Friedrich D. E. *Brief Outline of the Study of Theology.* Terrence N. Tice, trans. Richmond: John Knox, 1965.

_____. *The Christian Faith.* H. R. Mackintosh and J. S. Stewart, trans. Edinburgh: T. & T. Clark, 1928.

_____. *Der Christliche Glaube.* Seventh edition in two volumes. Martin Redeker, ed. Berlin: Walter de Gruyter & Co., 1960.

_____. *Die Christlich Sitte. Sämmtliche Werke*, Div. I, Vol. XII. L. Jonas, ed. Berlin: G. Reimer, 1843.

_____. *Dialektik. Sämmtliche Werke*, Div. III, Vol. IV, Pt. II. L. Jonas, ed. Berlin: G. Reimer, 1839.

_____. *Dialektik.* Rudolf Odebrecht, ed. Leipzig: J.C. Hinrichs, 1942.

_____. *Ethik (Entwürfe zu einem System der Sittenlenhre).* Vol. II of *Schleiermacher's Werke: Auswahl in vier Bänden.* Otto Braun and Johannes Bauer, eds. Leipzig: Felix Meiner, 1913.

_____. *Friedrich Schleiermacher's Sämmtliche Werke.* Thirty-one volumes. Berlin: G. Reimer, 1834-1864. Three basic divisions: I, theological; II, homiletical; III, philosophical.

_____. *Friedrich Schleiermacher's Werke: Auswahl in vier Bänden.* Otto Braun and Johannes Bauer, eds. Leipzig: Felix Meiner, 1910-1913.

_____. *Grundlinien einer Kritik der bisherigen Sittenlehre. Sämmtliche Werke*, Div. III, Vol. I. Berlin: G. Reimer, 1846.

_____. *Hermeneutik. Sämmtliche Werke*, Div. I, Vol. VII. Berlin: G. Reimer, 1838.

_____. *Kurze Darstellung des Spinozistischen Systems: Sämmtliche Werke*, Div. III, Vol. IV, Part I. Berlin: G. Reimer, 1839.

_____. *On Religion: Speeches to Its Cultured Despisers*. John Oman, trans. New York: Harper Torchbooks, 1958.

_____. *Psychologie. Sämmtliche Werke*, Div. III, Vol. VI. Berlin: G. Reimer, 1862.

_____. *Schleiermacher's Soliloquies*. Translation of the *Monologen*, with critical introduction and appendix, by Horace L. Friess. Chicago: Open Court, 1957.

_____. *Über die Religion: Reden an die Gebildeten unter ihren Verächtern*. Berlin: J. Friedrich Unger, 1799.

II. SECONDARY SOURCES

Augustine, Saint. *Basic Writings of Saint Augustine*. Whitney J. Oates, ed. New York: Random House, 1948.

Barth, Karl. *Church Dogmatics*, Vol. III, Part 3. G. W. Bromiley and T. F. Torrance, trans. Edinburgh: T. & T. Clark, 1958.

_____. *Protestant Thought: From Rousseau to Ritschl*. Brian Cozens, trans. New York: Simon and Schuster Clarion Book, 1959.

Birkner, Hans-Joachim. *Schleiermachers Christliche Sittenlehre*. Berlin: Verlag Alfred Töpelman, 1964.

Boyd, George N. "The Doctrine of Original Sin and the Fall in the Theology of Friedrich Schleiermacher." Th.D. diss., Union Theological Seminary, New York, 1970.

Brandt, Richard B. *The Philosophy of Schleiermacher*. New York: Harper & Brothers, 1941.

Brunner, Emil. *Die Mystik und das Wort*. Tübingen: J. C. B. Mohr, 1924.

_____. *Revelation and Reason*. Olive Wyon, trans. Philadelphia: Westminster, 1946.

Dilthey, Wilhelm. *Leben Schleiermachers*. H. Mulert, ed. Second edition, revised. Berlin: Vereinigung wissenschaftlichen Verleger, 1922.

Dupré, Louis. "Toward a Revaluation of Schleiermacher's Philosophy of Religion," *Journal of Religion* 44:2 (April 1964): 97-112.

Farrer, Austin. *Love Almighty and Ills Unlimited: An Essay on Providence and Evil.* Garden City, New York: Doubleday & Co., 1961.

Ferré, Nels F. S. *Evil and the Christian Faith.* New York: Harper & Brothers, 1947.

Fischer, Hermann. *Subjektivität und Sünde: Kierkegaards Begriff der Sünde mit Ständiger Rücksicht auf Schleiermachers Lehre von der Sünde.* Itzehoe, Holstein: Verlag Die Spur, 1963.

Flückiger, Felix. *Philosophie und Theologie bei Schleiermacher.* Zurich: Evangelisher Verlag, 1947.

Forstman, Jack. "Barth, Schleiermacher and *The Christian Faith*," *Union Theological Seminary Quarterly Review* 21:3 (March 1966).

Friebel, Horst. *Die Beduetung des Bösens für die Entwicklung der Pädagogik Schleiermachers.* Ratingen bei Düsseldorf: A. Hehn Verlag, 1961.

Gilkey, Langdon. *Maker of Heaven and Earth.* Garden City NY: Doubleday, 1959.

Harvey, Van A. "A Word in Defense of Schleiermacher's Theological Method," *Journal of Religion* 42:3 (July 1962): 151-70.

———. *The Historian and the Believer.* New York: Macmillan, 1966.

Heidegger, Martin. *Sein und Zeit.* Halle: Max Niemeyer Verlag, 1927.

Hick, John. *Evil and the God of Love.* New York: Harper & Row, 1966.

Joad, C. E. M. *God and Evil.* New York: Harper & Brothers, 1943.

Jorgensen, Paul. *Die Ethik Schleiermachers.* München: Chr. Kaiser Verlag, 1959.

Kaufmann, Gordon D. *Systematic Theology: A Historicist Perspective.* New York: Scribner's, 1968.

Laist, Bruno. *Das Problem der Abhängigkeit in Schleiermachers Anthropologie und Bildungslehre.* Ratingen bei Düsseldorf: A. Henn Verlag, 1965.

Lehmann, Paul L. *Ethics in a Christian Context.* New York: Harper & Row, 1963.

Mackintosh, Hugh R. *Types of Modern Theology.* New York: Scribner's, 1937.

Macquarrie, John. *An Existentialist Theology: A Comparison of Heidegger and Bultmann.* New York: Harper Torchbooks, 1965.

_____. *Principles of Christian Theology*, second edition. New York: Scribner's, 1977.

Niebuhr, H. Richard. *Christ and Culture.* New York: Harper & Row, 1951.

Niebuhr, Reinhold. *The Nature and Destiny of Man.* Two volumes. New York: Scribner's, 1941.

Niebuhr, Richard R. *Schleiermacher on Christ and Religion.* New York: Scribner's, 1964.

Ogden, Schubert M. *The Reality of God.* New York: Harper & Row, 1963.

Otto, Rudolph. *The Idea of The Holy.* J. Harvey, trans. London: Oxford University, 1970.

Ricoeur, Paul and Alastair MacIntyre. *The Religious Significance of Atheism.* New York: Columbia University, 1969.

Ricoeur, Paul. *The Symbolism of Evil.* Emerson Buchanan, trans. Boston: Beacon, 1969.

Robinson, James M. and John B. Cobb, Jr., eds. *The New Hermeneutic.* New York: Harper & Row, 1964.

Sartre, Jean-Paul. *The Transcendence of the Ego.* F. Williams and R. Kirkpatrick, trans. New York: Noonday, 1957.

Schenk, H. G. *The Mind of the European Romantics.* New York: Doubleday, 1969.

Selbie, W. B. *Schleiermacher.* London: Chapman & Hall, 1913.

Spiegler, Gerhard. *The Eternal Covenant.* New York: Harper & Row, 1967.

Tice, Terrence N. *Schleiermacher Bibliography.* Princeton Pamphlets, 12. Princeton NJ: Princeton Theological Seminary, 1966.

Tillich, Paul. *Perspectives on Nineteenth and Twentieth Century Protestant Theology.* Carl E. Braaten, ed. New York: Harper and Row, 1967.

_____. *Systematic Theology.* Three volumes in one. Chicago: University of Chicago, 1967.

Wagner, Falk. *Schleiermacher's Dialektik: Eine Kritische Interpretation.* Gütersloh: Gütersloher Verlagshaus Gerd Mohn, 1974.

Williams, Robert R. "Consciousness and Redemption in the Theology of Friedrich Schleiermacher." Th.D. diss., Union Theological Seminary, New York, 1971.

Wittgenstein, Ludwig. *Tractatus Logico-Philosophicus.* London: Kegan Paul, Trench, Trubner & Co., 1922.

Zahrnt, Heinz. *The Question of God: Protestant Theology in the Twentieth Century.* R. A. Wilson, trans. New York: Harcourt Brace Jovanovich, 1969.

NABPR DISSERTATION SERIES

The National Association of Baptist Professors of Religion was organized in 1981 to promote communication and cooperation among professors of religion. The Association publishes a scholarly quarterly journal, *Perspectives in Religious Studies*, a Bibliographic Series, and a Special Studies Series in addition to the Dissertation Series. Titles in the Dissertation Series are listed below.

1. Timothy George, *John Robinson and the English Separatist Tradition*. Macon, GA: Mercer University Press, 1982.

2. Victor A. Shepherd, *The Nature and Function of Faith in the Theology of John Calvin*. Macon, GA: Mercer University Press, 1983.

3. Claude Y. Stewart, Jr., *Nature in Grace: A Study in the Theology of Nature*. Macon, GA: Mercer University Press, 1983.

4. Stanley Grenz, *Isaac Backus—Puritan and Baptist*. Macon, GA: Mercer University Press, 1983.

5. David Paul Henry, *The Early Development of the Hermeneutic of Karl Barth as Evidenced by His Appropriation of Romans 5:12-21*. Macon, GA: Mercer University Press, 1985.

6. John William Beaudean, Jr., *Paul's Theology of Preaching*. Macon, GA: Mercer University Press, 1988.

7. John Sykes, *The Romance of Innocence and the Myth of History: Faulkner's Religious Critique of Southern Culture*. Macon, GA: Mercer University Press, 1989.

8. Michael Schuldiner, *Gifts and Works: The Post Conversion Paradigm and Spiritual Controversy in Seventeenth-Century Massachusetts*. Macon, GA: Mercer University Press, 1991.

9. Molly Truman Marshall, *No Salvation outside the Church? A Critical Inquiry*. Lewiston, NY: The Edwin Mellen Press, 1993.

10. Dale F. Leschert, *Hermeneutical Foundations of Hebrews: A Study in the Validity of the Epistle's Interpretation of Some Core Citations from the Psalms*. Lewiston, NY: The Edwin Mellen Press, 1994.

11. Robert Lee Vance, *Sin and Self-Consciousness in the Thought of Friedrich Schleiermacher*. Lewiston, NY: The Edwin Mellen Press, 1994.

GENERAL THEOLOGICAL SEMINARY
NEW YORK